Lady Margaret Hall 400 yards
Wolfson College ¾ of a mile

D0803268

River Cherwell

MANSFIELD ROAD

University Museum

Rhodes Building

Mansfield College

St. Catherine's College

Wadham College

Manchester College

New Bodleian Library

Clarendon Building

Sheldonian Theatre

HOLYWELL STREET

Hertford College

New College

Exeter College

Divinity School

Bodleian Library

BRASENOSE LANE

All Souls College

Queen's College

St Edmund Hall

Brasenose College

Radcliffe Camera

St Mary's Church

Lincoln College

Magdalen College

All Saints' Church

HIGH STREET

University College

LOGIC LANE

Hall

Oriel College

MAGDALEN BRIDGE

Merton College

Botanic Gardens

City Wall

Christchurch College

Corpus Christi College

St Hilda's College

Christchurch Meadows

OXFORD & CAMBRIDGE

OXFORD & CAMBRIDGE

Richard Gloucester
Hermione Hobhouse

Thames and Hudson

First published in the United States in 1980 by Thames and Hudson, Inc.,
500 Fifth Avenue, New York, New York 10036.

**This book was designed and produced by
John Calmann & Cooper Limited, London**

Filmset by Southern Positives and Negatives (SPAN), Lingfield, Surrey.
Printed and bound in Great Britain by Morrison & Gibb Ltd., Edinburgh.

Library of Congress Catalog card number: 79-92415

1 (*Frontispiece*) **The Tower of
the Five Orders, Bodleian
Library, Oxford.**

CONTENTS

INTRODUCTION

OXFORD AND CAMBRIDGE are unique among the university towns of the world. Essentially two provincial cities, without medieval ruler or bishop, let alone a later prince of the enlightenment, their townscape is a by-product of an educational system. As an American wrote about Cambridge in the 1840s:

> Imagine the most irregular town that can be imagined, streets of the very crookedest kind, twisting about like those in a nightmare ... The houses are low and antique; sometimes their upper stories project out into and over the narrow pathway ...
>
> Among these narrow, ugly and dirty streets, are tumbled in, as it were at random some of the most beautiful academical buildings in the world ...[1]

Modern town planners have done their best to codify the results and to rationalize suggestions for the future, but the development of the two cities is essentially a product of *laisser-faire* and of rivalry. Alone amongst the medieval universities of Europe they have preserved the collegiate system. This has endured for over six centuries, suffering change often grudgingly and with an ill grace, but its survival has proved what a surprisingly durable system it is.

The essence of the system is the college and, within the college, the court or quadrangle. In Sir Nikolaus Pevsner's words: 'whatever the quality of the single units, it is the way they make up into courts, large and small, and colleges and groups of colleges and ultimately architecture and landscape, that matters ...'

For 600 years men have been planning and designing and building colleges, so that today, in spite of traffic congestion, pollution and other urban ills, Oxford and Cambridge are two of the most architecturally exciting places in the world.

What led their founders and benefactors to create such a series of masterpieces: was it *ad majorem dei gloriam?* was it to improve the quality of clergy or civil servants? was it to enhance the national standing in the sciences, in economics, or in agriculture? or was it perhaps emulation – a desire to outdo other institutions, other statesmen, to elevate one's own profession, one's own countrymen, one's own county, or more particularly one's own college above rivals? On the other hand, many of the universities' greatest benefactors were never undergraduates there, and they seem to attract generosity and inspire enthusiasm from all fields of human achievement.

This book is an attempt to show the results of such benefaction and enthusiasms, and to try to explain how it was translated into magnificent buildings.

2 The gates at the back of Clare College, Cambridge.

3 The cupolas of Queen's College, seen from University College.

4 Looking down into Gonville and Caius College and Trinity Great Court from the tower of Great St Mary's church.

5 (overleaf) King's College and Clare from the Backs.

OXFORD

Medieval Oxford

Oxford was a thriving community before the arrival of any scholars, thanks to its important strategic and commercial position astride the Thames at its junction with the Cherwell. Not only was there a fine safe ford for the traveller, but the town grew up at the crossing of two important routes: the north-south route which connected the Midlands with Southampton and the crossing to France, and the military road from London to the Welsh Marches and Gloucester. Both these routes fostered the growth of the university in due course, making the town easily accessible to both native and foreign scholars.

There is some doubt about the date at which the Abbey of St Frideswide was founded, but it is probably Anglo-Saxon in origin. The Anglo-Saxon Chronicle mentioned Oxford as a community of importance in the tenth century, and the Normans recognized its importance by establishing a castle there within a decade of the Conquest. Henry I built Beaumont Palace there in the eleventh century, starting a royal connection with Oxford which reached its climax in Stuart times.

Like other institutions, Oxford University has flirted with agreeable fictions about its origins – University College long claimed Alfred the Great as founder – but it is now accepted that its emergence as a *studium generale* dates from the twelfth century. There was already a community of scholars in Oxford, but the establishment of a recognized educational centre with several faculties and a number of masters only followed on the migration of a group of scholars from Paris in 1167. There were at this period several other English schools of importance including the cathedral cities of York, Hereford and Lincoln and, for a brief period, Stamford and Northampton. Oxford was the centre which survived. A number of theories have been put forward to explain this, one suggesting that it is the result of its excellent strategic position, another that it is because of the royal presence at Woodstock and in Oxford itself. Although there was no medieval bishopric of Oxford, the university came under the control and protection of the Bishop of Lincoln, who assisted the young academic community in its struggle with the townsfolk.

The recurrent battle between students and townspeople seem always to have benefited the university. In 1209, a riot resulted in the university being closed for several years, but when it reassembled in 1214 it was with the benefit of a papal charter giving the academic authorities complete control over all the scholars. In addition, the town was obliged to pay compensation of fifty-two shillings a year to the university. This settlement of 1214 is particularly important because it brought the University Chest, or treasury, into being to administer this compensation, and also because it contains the first mention of the Chancellor. This official was the administrator of the

6 St John's College, Oxford.

7 and 8 *(left)* **The Radcliffe Camera;** *(right)* **New College cloister.**

scholastic community, originally appointed by the Bishop of Lincoln, although, in due course, the masters gained the right to elect him themselves.

As a result of the settlement following the St Scholastica's Day riots of 1355, the University gained even more favourable terms: a new charter gave it control over markets, weights, measures and the quality of bread and ale. In addition, the Chancellor's courts henceforth claimed jurisdiction over all mixed disputes involving both townsmen and scholars.

Shortly after this the university freed itself from the suzerainty of the Bishop of Lincoln, who was forced to surrender his right of confirmation of the Chancellor in 1367, through the intervention of Pope Urban V. The university established its freedom from ecclesiastical control generally some thirty years later, emerging as an important self-governing corporation unshackled by either ecclesiastical or civic control.

Oxford was ruled by the Chancellor, who presided over the Congregation, the assembly of the masters. He was assisted by two proctors, who were elected annually – one by the southern masters (a division which included the Welsh and Irish masters) and the other by the northern. The Chancellor's court was responsible for law and order, and could both fine and imprison offenders. The licensing of masters to teach and the right of students to take their degrees was also under the control of the Chancellor. The masters of the university formed the Great Congregation which had the right to discuss and pass statutes for the governing of the university.

The *studium generale* can be seen as the precursor of the independent university and, in the same way, the hostel or hall foreshadowed the college. The early scholars lived in lodgings rented from the townspeople, with consequent friction, or in hostels or halls which were largely run by the teaching masters for their own students, not unlike the boarding houses run by nineteenth-century public school masters. Friars and monks sent to the university lived in daughter communities established by their orders for the purpose. Most of these communities disappeared at the Reformation, although part of the Benedictine foundation of Gloucester College (1283) survives in the buildings of modern Worcester College. Gloucester College was a hall supported jointly by a number of monasteries, each of which had its own *camera* for students, 'divided', in the words of Anthony á Wood, 'though all for the most part adjoining each other, by particular roofs, partitions and various forms of structure, and known from each other, like so many colonies and tribes, by arms and rebuses that are depicted and cut in stone over each door.'

Other monastic communities were Durham College, later re-founded as Trinity, and St Bernard College, whose buildings provided the nucleus for St John's. The different orders of friars were very active at Oxford: the Carmelites were granted the royal palace of Beaumont, while the Franciscans gave Oxford a number of her most distinguished medieval scholars in Roger Bacon, Duns Scotus and William of Ockham.

The first colleges, that is self-governing independent communities, usually with their own statutes, appeared at the end of the thirteenth century. They seem to have been modelled on the colleges already in existence at Paris University. They were founded by wealthy benefactors, anxious to help poor scholars, but also concerned to leave a fine monument and to establish a form of chantry, where chaplains would say masses for the benefit of their souls. These foundations were often very modest with only a small number of masters and scholars supported by the foundation, but their numbers were swelled by others who came to live there as boarders, these latter culminating in the elegant Gentleman-Commoners of nineteenth-century Oxford.

University College claims to be the oldest, because it was founded on the bequest of William of Durham in 1249, although it only found a home in the High Street in 1280. Balliol was established through the benefactions of John of Balliol and his Scottish wife slightly earlier, on a site outside the north gate of the city, beside the town moat which was later filled in to form Broad Street.

Merton College, founded in 1262 by Walter de Merton, Chancellor of England, was the largest and wealthiest of the early colleges, supporting some 40 fellows and 25 scholars. Its magnificent and ambitious buildings have fortunately survived, including the great hall of 1277, the fourteenth-century Mob Quad, and its original library. The great chapel, begun in 1290, is of particular interest since it is only part of what was planned. It was intended to have a nave and aisles, making it larger than many priory churches. In fact only the choir, crossing and transepts were built making it the prototype for all Oxford college chapels, a building type unique to Oxford, and only introduced to Cambridge at St John's Chapel in 1863 by Sir George Gilbert Scott. The quadrangle, too, set a pattern as it was the first to be planned as such.

Four more colleges were founded in the fourteenth century: Exeter (1314), founded by a Devonian for west country scholars; Oriel (1326); Queen's College (1341) established by Robert of Eglesfield, chaplain to the Queen, Philippa of Hainault, for north country students. The most magnificent was, however, William of Wykeham's New College, established to provide a university education for the boys who had been educated at the college he founded at Winchester. The buildings were designed by the same architect William Wynfold. It was a very large establishment for seventy scholars, including for the first time, undergraduates, the previous colleges having been for graduates studying for their doctorates. The scale of the foundation is demonstrated by the quadrangle laid out and built by 1400, containing all the major collegiate elements: chapel, hall, and quadrangle. An important element was the entrance gateway, which both defended students against angry townspeople and also symbolized the restraint imposed on the students.

Control of a relatively large student population had always been a problem for the university authorities. Early attempts had included the obligation for every student to be enrolled with a teaching master. This had not been enough to prevent some of the worst excesses, or to control those 'persons who in the guise of scholars abide in divers places within the university and the precincts of the same, not residing in halls or having principals, who are called chamber dekenys and who sleep all day and at night lurk about taverns and brothels, bent on robbing and homicide.'[2] In 1410 a statute was passed to require all students to reside in a college or hall, and to ban them from lodging with townspeople.

This naturally increased the number of halls which already housed a much larger proportion of the students than the more luxurious colleges. There

9 The north range of Front Quad, Queen's College, built in 1714.

10 Worcester College showing the range built when the college was founded in 1714.

were as many as seventy halls in the mid-fifteenth century, but the number diminished rapidly thereafter as they were absorbed by colleges in the succeeding century and only eight remained by the middle of the sixteenth century. St Mary Hall and Bedel Hall were both absorbed by Oriel; others like Magdalen Hall and Hart Hall both survived into the nineteenth century to become Hertford College (1874). The only hall to survive into this century, St Edmund Hall, became a college in 1957.

The hall provided a central hall and buttery for the students and rooms, shared as in colleges, and usually consisting of a large central dormitory with studies off for private use. They lacked the endowment and the self-governing organization of the colleges, and as the tutorial system developed by which individual students each had their tutor, they were increasingly unable to match the facilities offered to students.

The fifteenth century was a period of architectural achievement against an uneasy background of civil strife and religious dissension. The three colleges founded in that century epitomize these characteristics: Lincoln in the Turl was founded by Richard Fleming, another Bishop of Lincoln, to provide scholars who would fight Lollardy. Always a poor college, it has preserved its original fifteenth-century Front Quad and much of the early work on its Brasenose Lane frontage.

All Souls' College was a much richer foundation, founded by Henry Chichele, Archbishop of Canterbury, with Henry VI as co-founder. It takes its name from its chantry function of praying for the 'souls of the faithful departed', particularly Henry V and those who died in the Hundred Years' War. It was to support a warden and forty fellows, and alone among the older colleges at Oxford has never admitted undergraduates.

The third college was Magdalen, 'of all Oxford colleges, the stateliest and most secluded from the world'. It was founded by William of Waynflete, also Lord High Chancellor of England, and himself a product of Winchester and New College. He gave the new college a close connection with the new foundation of Eton College, making provision for twenty-five upper-class students annually to share studies with the poor scholars and those destined for the church, an important acknowledgement of the way in which university education was to become increasingly secular.

The university buildings as such were relatively modest at the end of the Middle Ages compared to such magnificently equipped and endowed institutions as New College, Merton and All Souls. St Mary's Church, in the High Street, was the first university building as such, already acknowledged in the fourteenth century as the university church – St Martin's Church at Carfax, now only a truncated tower, was the City's. In 1320 a congregation house was built on the north side with a room above used for the university's first collection of books given by Bishop Cobham in 1327.

Tudor and Stuart Oxford

The Renaissance brought many changes to the universities: in the field of studies, even more in the type of undergraduate attracted, and also in the organization of university and college.

The curriculum had already begun to change: the medieval student had faced a gruelling course. He studied for seven years for the Master's degree, including the *Trivium* – Latin grammar, Logic and Rhetoric – and then the *Quadrivium*, which consisted of Arithmetic, Geometry, Astronomy and Music, followed by Hebrew and Greek Philosophy and History. Only after he had attained his Master's degree could he proceed to a Doctorate in Theology, Law or Medicine, which took a further nine years' study. This ensured that only those who intended to enter the church or to lead a life of scholarship attended the universities.

In 1431, the university authorities reorganized the lectures given by the regents or teaching masters to make them more useful to students. There were ten fields of study: the seven liberal arts, and the three philosophies, moral, natural and metaphysical. Although the emphasis was still on the study of law and theology, the gift of Duke Humphrey's manuscripts meant that the new learning from Byzantium was available to Oxford scholars. Greek and Hellenic culture began to be studied at Oxford, not only through manuscripts but through the teaching of scholars who had been to Padua and other Italian universities.

With the invention of printing, books became more widely available and libraries ceased to be the perquisite of rich institutions. The publication of modern authors like Erasmus became possible and this, in an age of controversy, stimulated discussion and thought.

The first book was printed at Oxford in 1478, but the University Press only really came into being after the Restoration. Printing was carried out in the basement of the Sheldonian, but in 1713 it was moved to the new Clarendon Building, taking its name from the author of the *History of the Great Rebellion*, the profits from which provided the Press with a home.

Oxford was no more successful with its first library than with its early printing. In 1420 the university decided to build the Divinity Schools, now part of the Bodleian complex, and, in token of gratitude to Humphrey, Duke of Gloucester, suggested that the new library to be incorporated in the building should be named after him. The Divinity School with its vaulted roof is, in Pevsner's words, 'one of the marvels of Oxford', and Duke Humphrey's library above was at the time one of the great glories of the university.

The early part of the fifteenth century was a period of growth with no less than three colleges being established. Brasenose College, better known as BNC, was founded on the ancient building of Brasenose Hall in the High Street by William Smyth, Bishop of Lincoln. The college could only afford a quadrangle in the early years, and chapel and library were added 150 years later. The larger New Quad on the High Street was added by T. G. Jackson at the end of the nineteenth century in sensitive early Arts and Crafts Gothic. This tradition of intelligent architectural patronage has been continued in the recent Powell and Moya building.

Corpus Christi was founded by the Master of Pembroke College, a former Magdalen man who was obviously anxious to spread its tradition of classical learning. Corpus was founded with a President, Professors of Theology, Greek and Latin, whose lectures were to benefit the whole university, twenty Fellows and twenty scholars. Modest in size though it was, the new college was typical of the new Oxford – outgoing, humanistic, rejecting the narrow medieval form of a chantry college concerned with its own members and with the salvation of its founder's soul.

The greatest of the three was founded by another Chancellor of England, the last of the great prelate statesmen of the medieval tradition, Thomas Wolsey, Cardinal Archbishop of York. In 1525 he obtained a royal licence to found Cardinal College, using the revenues of the suppressed monastery of St Frideswide. The original intention was to demolish the whole of the Norman priory buildings, but at first only the western end of the church was demolished to make room for what was to be, and indeed remains, the largest quad in Oxford. Only the hall, together with the south side of the quad and the great kitchens, were completed by the time of Wolsey's fall; the other ranges and the cloisters had only been started. It was King Henry VIII himself who completed Wolsey's great scheme, reducing the proposed establishment from Dean and sixty canons to Dean and eight canons, together with 100 students. St Frideswide's truncated church was spared, and became Oxford's newly established Cathedral. Wolsey's projected great chapel was abandoned, and its site given over to canon's houses. Cardinal College became Christ Church, a well endowed royal foundation with revenues on the same vast scale as its sister foundation of Trinity College, Cambridge. It has remained the grandest and the most aristocratic, if not the most intellectual of Oxford Colleges. It possesses two important Gothic survivals, the vaulted roof of the hall staircase, designed in the mid-seventeenth century, and Wren's sympathetic completion of Tom Tower in 1681, designed in 'Gothic to agree with the Founder's work'. Further Gothic details were added by Bodley and Garner in the 1870s, considerably more sensitive and elegant than Deane's Meadow Buildings (1862–6).

The second great quad, Peckwater, was designed by the amateur, Henry Aldrich, Dean of Christ Church, at the beginning of the eighteenth century in an agreeable classical vernacular, almost calculated, one feels, to make those reared in Palladian country houses feel at home. An Archbishop of Armagh financed the building of Canterbury Quadrangle. Obliterating the fourteenth-century Canterbury College, it was designed by James Wyatt and intended to accommodate noblemen and gentlemen commoners.

The baroque library was designed by another Oxford architect, Dr George

Clarke of All Souls, and like the Wren Library at Trinity Cambridge was intended to be open on the ground floor. The magnificent first-floor library was complemented by an art gallery on the ground floor created to house a collection given to Christ Church in 1760–3. This collection was moved in 1967 to a new gallery, built by Powell and Moya in the Deanery garden.

In the unhappy middle years of the sixteenth century, the brief Counter-Reformation under Queen Mary left its mark on Oxford. Traditionally Roman Catholic and High Church, Royalist rather than Parliamentarian, Oxford could boast Sir Thomas More, Edmund Campion and Cardinal Pole, and later Archbishop Laud, as against the Cambridge Archbishops Parker and Whitgift. The Martyrs' Memorial, however, commemorates the burning of the three Cambridge Anglican churchmen, Latimer, Cranmer and Ridley, brought to Oxford for questioning, disputation and ultimate martyrdom in the Town Ditch, outside Balliol College.

Queen Mary's reign also saw the foundation of Trinity, incorporating the medieval buildings of Durham College, suppressed some ten years before. Little more was built until the next century, although the perfect baroque chapel attributed variously to Wren and Dean Aldrich justifies the lapse of a century. St John the Baptist's College inherited much more substantial buildings from the Cistercian College of St Bernard, founded by Archbishop Chichele in 1437 and suppressed in the 1540s. The college was refounded by Thomas White, a London merchant, who established a strong tradition of Catholicism and High Anglicanism, producing Anglican champions in Laud and Juxon, both Archbishops and benefactors of the college.

This thriving and intellectually stimulating period produced two more colleges. The first was the aggressively Protestant Jesus College, founded in 1571 to give the Welsh 'nation' a presence. The second was Wadham, established in 1610 by a Somerset gentleman sufficiently well-off to complete the college within three years, thus giving it a perfect set of Jacobean Gothic buildings.

The accession of Queen Elizabeth had ushered in a century of growth and prosperity for Oxford. The number of admissions increased, probably encouraged by the increasing ambition of every country gentleman to see his son an undergraduate. One authority calculates that yearly admissions rose from about 300 in the first decade of Elizabeth's reign to nearly 600 in 1630–9. Admissions did not at this period mean graduating but the number of those taking an Arts degree rose from about 123 in the 1570s to about double in 1611. The three centres of higher education, Oxford, Cambridge and the Inns of Court in London, were attended by a higher proportion of the university-age population during this period than at any time until after 1914. Significantly over half of the undergraduates came from the ranks of the country gentry. Oxford had become a lay university although there was still a large number of students destined for the Church of England.

The curriculum had been considerably shortened to four years, except for the sons of peers and knights, who were allowed to complete it in three. The student still demonstrated his progress through a series of disputations, often on subjects drawn from Aristotelian philosophy. Nonetheless, the professorships founded in the early seventeenth century indicated a widening field of scholarship. Chairs of astronomy, geometry, and natural philosophy were

11 Heads of Roman Emperors outside the Sheldonian Theatre. The Old Clarendon Building is in the background.

endowed, while in 1621 the Botanic Gardens, essential for the study of medicine and botany, were laid out. Ancient history, music and Arabic were other specialized fields.

This was a period of growth not only in university posts but in university buildings. The Divinity Schools with Duke Humphrey's Library above it were the first purpose-built university buildings. But in the uneasy times of the Reformation, the commissioners of Edward VI (1547–53) had pillaged the university library as pitilessly as their predecessors had those of the monasteries. By the end of the century the library was empty, bare even of shelves, and it was only through the efforts of Sir Thomas Bodley, a retired diplomat, that it was restored and re-stocked.

By 1602 the library was ready, the collection enhanced and a new librarian appointed. It was Bodley who came to the arrangement with the Stationers' Company by which a copy of each book printed was sent to the Bodleian, an arrangement later embodied in law. The endowment of books was so generous that by 1610 the building needed extension, and the 'Arts End' was added. His final benefaction was the building of the new Schools, completed in 1624, with its great Tower of the Five Orders, proclaiming its humanist learning.

The 'university site' at the end of Broad Street represented the only physical presence of the university itself. Three more important buildings were added during Stuart times. The first was, of course, the Sheldonian Theatre, designed by Sir Christopher Wren in 1664–9 and built to house ceremonies like *Encaenia*, hitherto performed in the nave of St Mary's church.

The growing importance of the natural sciences was shown by the bequest in 1677 of the Tradescant collection to the university by Elias Ashmole. The Ashmolean museum was built to house it, remaining the repository of the university treasures until the New Ashmolean was opened in 1840. The last of this baroque group was the Clarendon Building. The old Ashmolean has been called the first modern museum because of the comprehensive nature of its collections, originating in the collection of the traveller and naturalist, John Tradescant of Lambeth (d. 1638), which was later bought by Ashmole. The original building contained a chemical laboratory, a lecture room and a library, in addition to the galleries for the display of the 'twelve cartloads of rarities'.

Archbishop Laud became Chancellor of Oxford in 1630. He had been President of St John's College from 1611–21 and had built its Canterbury Quad, the most impressive building of its date, according to Pevsner. Although the office had become more honorific, the day-to-day duties being discharged by a vice-chancellor who was drawn in rotation from among the heads of Houses, it was still possible for the busy chancellor to inculcate a number of significant changes. The high Anglicans were well aware of the need to purge the universities on the one hand of Popery, and on the other of contentious and subversive Puritans. With characteristic attention to detail Laud ordered the lives of undergraduate and don, as harsh towards foppish clothing and long hair as towards seditious and unorthodox preaching. The Laudian reforms were nonetheless valuable, and provided the rules for university life until the drastic reforms of 1854. One significant statute insisted on residence in some recognized college or hall for every undergraduate, which gave the existing institutions an effective monopoly, and indeed increased the power of the colleges vis-à-vis the University. Only in 1854 were private hostels allowed again, in the words of one contemporary, 'opening the university to the nation at large'.

Laud went on his fussy way to the Archbishopric of Canterbury and martyrdom, leaving Oxford, according to Clarendon, 'the only city of England entirely devoted to the King'. Loyalty to the King was a mixed blessing; many colleges gave their plate to be melted down for his treasury, and indeed few now possess any of the sumptuous pre-Civil-War plate. Although few undergraduates were in residence members of colleges were turned out for

12 The Front Quad of Wadham College, built in 1610–3. The chapel is on the left and the hall on the right of the central tower.

the benefit of courtiers and their ladies, and this was bitterly resented:

> The greater sort of the courtiers were high, proud, insolent, and looked upon scolars noe more than pedants, or pedagocicall persons: the lower sort also made noe more of them then the greater, not suffering them to see the king or queen at dinner or supper or scarce at cards or at masse, never regarding that they had parted with their chambers and conveniences.[3]

Not all the great ladies and gentlemen were housed in colleges. Lady Fanshawe complained that she and her sister:

> ... from as good a house as any gentleman of England had, we came to a baker's house in an obscure street, ... to lie in a very bad bed in a garret, to one dish of meat, and that not the best ordered, no money for we were as poor as Job; at the windows the sad spectacle of war, sometimes plague, sometimes sickness of other kinds....[4]

The fortunes of war were reflected in the Chancellorship, held successively by Cromwell himself, and then by Lord Clarendon, reflecting the importance of a well-disposed Oxford to the government of the day. With the re-establishment of the Stuart dynasty, and the triumph of the Anglican church over republicans and non-conformists, Oxford's traditional leanings towards Crown and Church were given full reign. It was to Oxford that Charles II brought his Parliament in 1681, lodging at the royal foundation of Christ Church, although it was a relatively short session despite the university's loyalty. James II's attempts to install a sympathetic President of Magdalen, which did much to alienate a Royalist stronghold, was a total failure although he did succeed in appointing a Roman Catholic as Master of University College. Nonetheless, after the revolution of 1688 in which he was deposed in favour of his daughter Mary and her Dutch husband William III, a number of Oxford fellows joined the 'non-juring' clergy of the Church of England, finding a Dutch Presbyterian on the throne of England impossible to stomach. Queen Anne was more to Oxford's taste, and the university split between whiggism and toryism, some colleges favouring the low Church party, others, notably Christ Church, adhering to a loyalist tradition.

With the accession of George I in 1714, the university entered on a period of disfavour and indeed active distrust on the part of the Whig government – unlike its sister university:

> King George, observing with judicious eyes
> The state of both his universities,
> To Oxford sent a troop of horse; and why?
> That learned body wanted loyalty.
> To Cambridge books he sent, as well discerning
> How much that loyal body wanted learning.[5]

Unreformed Oxford

The eighteenth century left its mark on Oxford in the field of architecture rather than that of learning or academic advance. Colleges and fellows both grew comfortable on endowments. The livings of a rich college like Merton went to its favourite sons, while the fellows of Magdalen and Christ Church embellished their buildings.

The wealthy gentleman-commoners, with 'their very rich lace, red stockings, silver-buttoned coats and other things which constitute a man of taste in Oxford', were features of fashionable colleges. Their status and boarding fees entitled them to wear an elegant silk gown and to dine with the fellows. Ordinary commoners were more modest figures wearing the ridiculous short gowns which have survived; those too poor to be com-moners, and unable to achieve a scholarship, could attend the university as a servitor, inhabiting the least desirable rooms and carrying out menial duties within the college.

Life was not elegant, even in the richer colleges: a German visitor to Christ Church in 1710 wrote in disgust:

> Hall, exceedingly large and lofty, but otherwise mean and ugly; there was such a stench of bread and meat, that I was driven out; I could not eat or live in such a place. Our disgust was increased by the coarse and filthy tablecloths, the square wooden trenchers and platters to receive the bones ... Both *socii collegiorum* and students or scholars dine here; those of quality dine in their rooms...[6]

The tutorial system already existed by which each undergraduate had a senior member of the college, with whom he did a certain amount of reading, who was responsible for his debts, and up to a point for his morals. A tutor could, if he were a conscientious and educated man, influence his pupils considerably. Lord Shelburne recalled his tutor as 'not without learning and [he] certainly set himself out to be serviceable to me in point of reading. I read with him a good deal of natural law, and the law of nations, some history, part of Livy, and translated some of the Orations of Demosthenes with tolerable care.'[7]

The college tutor was not, however, always available to teach his undergraduates, and by the nineteenth century a system of private tuition had grown up. The private tutor was often a sort of crammer resorted to immediately before an examination was taken, efficacious but expensive. Examinations still took the form of disputations, and candidates had to go through the formality of disputing, often, according to an eighteenth-century critic, the worst sort of farce:

> These [arguments] are always handed down from generation to gene-ration, on long slips of paper, and consist of foolish syllogisms on foolish subjects ... the examiners and the candidates often converse on the last drinking bout, or on horses, or read the newspaper, or a novel, or divert themselves as well as they can ... until the clock strikes....[8]

There were, of course, studious and scholarly members of the university, but also a number for whom passing the time agreeably in sporting pursuits was more important. Organized sports were a largely nineteenth-century development; the first Boat Race was rowed at Henley in 1829, attended by the undergraduate Gladstone, but hunting, shooting and beagling were common amusements, with the river a constant resource in the summer.

The city itself, like so many English towns, was probably at its most picturesque and attractive at the beginning of the nineteenth century. The previous century had seen the addition of a number of important buildings, notably the triple donation of Dr Radcliffe – the Observatory, the Infirmary and, perhaps most elegant of the University's own buildings, the Camera. The High Street had been enriched by Queen's Front Quad, by Hawksmoor's towers for the North Quad of All Souls, and by the preaching box of All Saints' Church. The High Street is always said to have been the inspiration of Nash's Regent Street, its distinct but homogeneous elements providing a precedent for Burton's and Soane's commercial blocks, while Aldrich's spire gave an even more obvious pattern for the absurd topknot of All Souls', Langham Place.

It was a period at which perhaps town and gown were physically in balance. But with the thrusting expansion of the Victorian age, as much physical as intellectual, the university came to swamp the town. A Victorian don looking back lamented the loss of the commercial High Street shops:

> From Coach and Horse Lane to the Angel stretched a great block of shops, swept away to make room for the new Schools.... The Angel was the fashionable hotel: the carriages and four of neighbouring magnates, the Dukes of Marlborough and Buckingham, Lords Macclesfield, Abingdon, Camoys, dashed up to it; there too stopped all day post-chaises, travelling chariots, equipages of bridal couples, coaches from the eastern road; all ... being received at the hall door by the obsequious manager, in blue tail coat gilt buttoned and velvet collared, buff waistcoat, light kerseymere pantaloons, silk stockings and pumps....[9]

In those pre-railway days, visitors also used the river. When the Lord Mayor of London came to Oxford on a state visit in 1826, he brought his State Barge, complete with scarlet banners and liveried boatmen. The Oxford Canal was built to link the navigable Thames to the canal system of the Midlands at Rugby, and was a vital part of the transport network until the development of the railways.

When the City of London Companies gave up their State Barges, the stately monsters moved up-river to provide grandstands for the newly fashionable sport of rowing. In 1846 the recently founded University Boat Club acquired the Merchant Taylors' Barge; in 1859, Balliol purchased that of the Skinners' Company, while other colleges were content with copies. It was, of course, from the barges that the undergraduates drowned themselves for love of Zuleika Dobson. The barges, themselves no mean feats of architecture and rich in the rebuses and heraldic devices which have survived almost to excess in Oxford, proved expensive to maintain, and were gradually abandoned in favour of brick-built boathouses after the Great War.

In the 1830s, recalled the same nostalgic don, it was said that:

> the approach to Oxford by the Henley road was the most beautiful in the world. Soon after passing Littlemore you came in sight of ... the sweet city with its dreaming spires, driven along a road now crowded and obscured with dwellings, open then to cornfields on the right, to unenclosed meadows on the left, with an unbroken view of the long line of towers, rising out of foliage less high and veiling than after sixty more years of

growth today. At once, without suburban interval, you entered the finest quarter of the town, rolling under Magdalen Tower, and past the Magdalen elms, then in full unmutilated luxuriance, till the exquisite curves of the High Street opened on you, as you drew up at the Angel, or passed on to the Mitre and the Star. Along that road, or into Oxford by the St Giles's entrance, lumbered at midnight Pickford's vast waggons with their six musically belled horses; sped stage-coaches all day long....[10]

All this activity disappeared with the advent of the railways in 1844, the Great Western station being built on the site of Osney Abbey, the London Midland and Scottish terminating on that of the rather later foundation of Rewley. There is still a glimpse of towers – between the gasworks and the station, although the latter has now been rebuilt.

A bird's eye view of the 1850s shows how much the university still dominated the city, which was bounded by the Meadows on the south, by Magdalen Bridge on the east, with little building between Wadham and the University Parks to the north. Only to the west did the town sprawl away beyond Worcester College and Carfax. To the north lay St Giles's, the site of the annual Fair, but all was rural north of St John's. All this was to change as the reformed university expanded into new fields of study, building museums, new departments, and also new colleges to house Tractarians, nonconformists and ultimately women, all students unthought of and indeed actively discouraged in the latitudinarian days of Hanoverian Oxford.

Reform and Revolution: 19th century Oxford

The University over which the Duke of Wellington was installed in 1834 owned undissolved continuity with the Oxford of Addison, Thomas Hearne, the Wartons, Bishop Lowth; the seeds of the changes which awaited it – of Church movements, Museums and Art Galleries, Local Examinations, Science Degrees, Extension Lectures, Women's Colleges – germinating unsuspected while the old warrior was emitting his genial false quantities in the Theatre....[11]

Some of these challenges came from outside in the shape of the competition from other centres of higher education like University College, London, founded in 1836, with its atheistic flavour, and nonconformist centres like Manchester and Birmingham, with their local colleges. The Charity Commissioners' long hard look at educational charities throughout the country had inevitable repercussions on the standards of higher education. The heads of the reformed public schools and grammar schools fuelled the reform movement with their concern for the success and welfare of their ex-pupils.

Other movements were almost home-grown: the Oxford Movement, although not exclusively confined to the older university, found its natural breeding-ground amongst the High Church sympathizers. Newman served his first curacy in a church near the Plain (not far from Magdalen), and Matthew Arnold recalled his preaching in St Mary's:

Who could resist the charm of that spiritual apparition gliding in the dim afternoon light through the aisles of St Mary's, rising into the pulpit, and ...

in the most entrancing of voices, breaking the silence with words and thoughts which were as religious music – subtle, sweet, mournful?

Not all High Church Oxonians followed Newman into the Roman fold, and the foundation of Keble College in 1866 to commemorate John Keble shows the strength of the Tractarian movement even after the defection of Newman and others. There was also a strong Evangelical party in the university, and both lots of churchmen were worried by a strong radical challenge which wished to open the university to non-members of the Church of England, to reduce the exclusive power of the colleges by providing for non-resident students, to make fellowships more freely available, to allow fellows to marry, and to widen the syllabus to include law, history, the natural sciences and mathematics. W. E. Gladstone was elected to the university seat in 1847, on the strength of the liberal interest, and proved a conciliatory MP in the negotiations for a bill to reform the university in the 1850s.

Reform was only too obviously necessary: Pattison, a mild liberal who became Rector of Lincoln in due course, described the college in 1839:

> If you divide the Oxford Common Rooms into three classes, the first containing those whose members are Scholars and Divines – the second, which are fashionable, aristocratically inclined men of the world – the third unfashionable good homely squires, barristers, country parsons, – Oriel may be the instance of the first – Merton or All Souls of the second – and Lincoln will represent the third. To be more particular, the corporeal stature of the Fellows is large, their intellectual small....[12]

A royal commission was appointed in 1850 to examine the problems and the possibilities of reform, and duly reported two years later. Lord John Russell introduced a bill to remedy the abuses revealed by the report but was persuaded by Gladstone to accept a less draconian solution. In the event the Oxford University Reform Act revised the constitution but dealt with the major problem of reforming the colleges by appointing Commissioners to supervise the revision of the colleges' statutes. The new Hebdomadal Council was to consist of the Vice-Chancellor and the two proctors, long responsible for university discipline, six Heads of Colleges, six Professors and six members of Convocation elected by the MAs actively involved in teaching. This tilted the balance towards the teaching members of the university.

The liberals won an early victory when the university was opened to dissenters, but religious tests were not finally abandoned until 1871. Even in 1861, nearly three-quarters of graduates took orders.

Reform came slowly to the university partly because of the entrenched position of heads of colleges, and the apparent longevity of conservative senior members of the university. Even so, the physical effect of these changes on the town of Oxford was enormous. The most obvious geographical symbol was the growth of North Oxford to accommodate the homes and families of married dons after celibacy was gradually abandoned. Throughout the city considerable architectural improvements took place.

The private halls, whose inmates were, in the words of a contemporary, 'the outcasts of more orderly colleges', and where 'the cost of living was enormous', were virtually abolished after 1850, despite the arrangements for

allowing the opening of new institutions. In fact, the remaining old halls were gradually taken over by colleges. St Edmund's Hall passed through a period of subservience to Queen's, but alone survived as a separate institution. St Mary Hall became part of Oriel, finally absorbed in 1902; New Inn Hall was taken over by Balliol and St Alban Hall by Merton. Magdalen Hall, which had been re-housed at Hart Hall after its own buildings were burnt in 1820, became Hertford College in 1874 through the generosity of the banker Thomas Baring. The rebuilding and extension of the college buildings gave Thomas Graham Jackson one of his greatest opportunities, using Renaissance and Palladian motifs to unite old and new buildings.

Nonconformist colleges, founded elsewhere, moved their headquarters to Oxford: Mansfield from Birmingham was Congregational; Manchester was for Unitarians, who were transferred from thence in 1889, naturally enough employing the Mancunian architect Worthington on their new home.

The advent of women was regarded with scarcely less horror by some High Churchmen. Pusey saw the women's colleges as 'one of the greatest misfortunes that has happened even in our own time in Oxford'. Once women were admitted, four colleges, Somerville and Lady Margaret Hall (1878), St Hugh's (1886) and St Hilda's (1893) were founded within fifteen years; but although women students were allowed to sit all university examinations by 1894 and were admitted to all colleges for lectures by 1906, they were only to take degrees in 1920. Until they were admitted as full members of the university, women's education was under the supervision of the Association

13 *(above left)* **The deer park in front of the New Buildings at Magdalen.**

14 *(above)* **The Bridge of Sighs designed by T. G. Jackson in 1913–4 to connect the two quads of Hertford College: the twentieth-century North Quad on the left, and on the right the classical remains of Magdalen Hall (1818–22).**

for the Higher Education of Women, one of whose early preoccupations was the provision of chaperones for women students attending lectures. Relatively small and impoverished, the women's colleges functioned from converted villas in North Oxford in the early years.

The older, richer colleges were not so inhibited from re-building operations. Balliol, long a leader in the academic field, being one of the first colleges to expect its undergraduates to go for a class rather than a pass degree, employed three extremely distinguished Gothicists to rebuild and modernize the college buildings, although elements by Henry Keene, James Wyatt and George Basevi Junior have survived. Salvin extended Wyatt's hall and added the buildings which bear his name in the 1850s, and Butterfield replaced the sixteenth-century chapel in 1856–7. Finally, the growth of the college under Jowett necessitated a new hall, designed by Waterhouse in the 1870s. Pevsner suggests kindly that the college was unlucky, and certainly Balliol lacks the self-confidence of Butterfield at Keble or the adroit historicism of Jackson at Hertford.

Sir George Gilbert Scott, with one of the most extensive practices of his generation, is well-represented at Oxford. He installed a rose window at the east end of the cathedral in the 1870s, added the Holywell range for New College and that on Broad Street for Exeter, and remodelled the chapels of New College and University College. His best-know work is probably the Martyrs' Memorial of 1841, although Exeter Chapel (1854–60), modelled on the Sainte-Chapelle, is perhaps even more striking.

Bodley and Garner were also well-patronized, both working at Christ Church, and building Magdalen's High Street gateway. Basil Champneys, fresh from Newnham College, Cambridge, worked for two new colleges, Somerville and Mansfield, but also extended Merton and New College, adding the 'gargantuan' Rhodes Building fronting the High Street at Oriel.

Most college chapels were restored to some degree, as were most ecclesiastical interiors elsewhere in the country, usually on sound ecclesiological lines. Decorative schemes were carried out by Burges at Worcester and Brasenose, and by Kempe at Pembroke (the former Broadgates Hall), in addition to full scale remodellings elsewhere. The names of well-known firms of ecclesiastical furnishers are pervasive at Oxford as elsewhere, and, of course, there were as well a number of new 'town churches' built to serve new suburbs. Oxford also had its share of those collegiate religious foundations which were such a feature of the Victorian religious revival.

The reforms of 1854 had only partially redressed the balance between the university and the colleges. The greatest disparity was in wealth: in 1874 the income of the colleges was £830,000, while that of the University as such was £32,000. It was difficult to ignore the Royal Commission of 1874 under its chairman, the Duke of Cleveland, when it recommended that a portion of the money spent by individual colleges on fellowships should go to the maintenance of university lecturers.

The second Reform Act, by putting greater emphasis on centrally controlled and organized courses, and providing the Common University Fund, created by a levy on colleges for the 'endowment of research', did much to decrease the independence of the colleges. This money went towards the payment of more professors, lecturers and readers as well as towards the endowment of libraries and facilities for research and apparatus. It was disbursed centrally through newly created boards of faculties, Theology, Law, Natural Sciences, and Arts. The greater variety and specialization of courses made it necessary for lectures to be shared and destroyed the old practice of self-contained tuition within each college. Even within colleges the character of fellowships changed. In 1852, before the first Reform Act, there had been about 500 fellowships, but this had fallen by the end of the 1870s to about 350. In addition, many colleges found it necessary to reform their statutes to attract enough fellows prepared to teach the undergraduates of the college, frequently by abandoning the requirement to be in holy orders and by giving them permission to live out of college and to marry. Even the headships of colleges went to laymen, except at Christ Church where the head of the college was also the Dean of the cathedral.

The Common University Fund was not intended to finance building but the inevitable result of the greater importance of the university was a growth in buildings. The New Ashmolean was erected in 1841–5, to the designs of C. R. Cockerell, to house the growing university collections and the Taylorian Institute for the teaching of modern languages.

The building of the Ashmolean for classical antiquities and works of art was followed by the further dispersal of the collection. The natural history specimens were transferred to a new site and a new building in Parks Road in 1860, which was designed by a young Irish architect, Benjamin Woodward. The interior itself is exemplary: the very columns are individual specimens of different types of marble, and the capitals are carved with flowers and foliage. Despite the patronage of Ruskin, and his avowed preference for older materials, the roof was of cast-iron and glass. This large polychromatic building, the symbol of modern scientific teaching at Oxford, was soon joined by a large number of specialist institutions, architecturally less flamboyant but perhaps more functional, which turned Parks Road into a university precinct.

Oxford in the twentieth century

You're reading History? A perfectly respectable school. The very worst is English literature and the next worst is Modern Greats. You want either a first or a fourth. There is no value in anything in between … Clothes. Dress as you do in a country house. Never wear a tweed coat and flannel trousers – always a suit. And go to a London tailor; you get better cut and longer credit.[13]

Superficially, the world of Evelyn Waugh's Sebastian Flyte was still the same as that of the Duke of Dorset in *Zuleika Dobson*; indeed elements of the pre-1914 world were to linger on into the post-war austerity of Cripps and Bevin. The relics of archaic, indeed Laudian, proctorial discipline remained into the 1950s in the regulations controlling the wearing of gowns to lectures and tutorials, and in those confining undergraduates to their own colleges between midnight and the early morning. Co-education only invaded the older colleges in the 1970s. New College, indeed, only admitted women in time for them to celebrate its sixth centenary in 1979.

15 Holywell Street.

In fact, many of these changes began immediately after the Armistice in 1919. As in other fields, the contribution of women to the war effort made the practical achievement of many of the pre-war suffragette goals relatively easy. In 1920 women undergraduates were allowed to matriculate and to take most degrees, although prejudice against their presence lingered on:

> The women ... run no tailors' bills in the High Street, but deck themselves in hairy woollens and shapeless tweeds ... Instead of a quiet pair of rooms, guarded by an impenetrable 'oak', upon a secluded staircase, each girl has a minute green-and-yellow bed-sitter opening off an echoing shiny corridor. Instead of deep sofas and coal fires, they have convertible divans and gas stoves. Instead of claret and port, they drink cocoa and Kia-Ora. Instead of the lordly breakfasts and lunches which a man can command in his own rooms, they are fed on warm cutlets and gravy off cold plates at a long table decked with daffodils.[14]

This account perhaps misread the effects of poverty as a form of choice. Male undergraduates too in the chill egalitarian world of the 1950s were to suffer in single bed-sitters without a kindly scout to clean up after them or their over-indulgent friends.

Emancipation of all undergraduates was hastened by the post-war influx of older students and this led to further attempts to bring the university up to date with the appointment of yet another Royal Commission. Its proposals were effected by the act of 1923, which made it compulsory for all undergraduates to take an examination to obtain entry. It also made it possible to pension off the older dons.

These changes were largely brought about by the poor financial situation of the university. Many of the colleges were primarily dependent on their agricultural estates whose revenues had never recovered from the slump of the 1870s, and their contribution to the university was nothing like large enough to support the laboratories and libraries which modern learning demanded. The first university grant made in the 1920s was a mere £30,000 a year, but it nonetheless gave rise to concern about academic freedom. In the 1970s the figure was nearly £13 million.

In fact, much of the twentieth-century endowment of Oxford has been due to private benefactors. One of the most munificent was Cecil Rhodes, founder of over 150 Rhodes scholarships, tenable at any college, although given an appropriate headquarters in Rhodes House, designed by the great imperialist's own chosen architect, Sir Herbert Baker. Rhodes brought scholars from North America, from all over what was then the British Empire, and even a number from Germany. Poorer indigenous scholars looked to local authorities rather than to private benefactors. The nineteenth-century reforms had seen the abolition of a number of college scholarships, but the balance was redressed by public educational authorities who financed those undergraduates clever enough to get a place but unable to get an open scholarship. By 1939, it was estimated that over half the undergraduates were assisted in some way.

The only college to be founded between the wars was post-graduate and co-educational. Nuffield College was founded in 1937, and the buildings were designed – and re-designed – before the outbreak of war, but building did not begin till 1949. The design was then the watered-down Cotswold favoured by the native founder William Morris, rather than the 'cross between a mosque and a public lavatory' of the first scheme produced by Austen Harrison, an architect best known for his work in inter-war Jerusalem.

Morris, the greatest native benefactor of the university, started his career selling bicycles in Longwall Street. He founded Morris Garages and then the car works at Cowley, which developed into a suburb which threatened both the university and the ancient city. He was extremely generous to the university, endowing a number of medical institutions, old and new, including the Radcliffe Infirmary and new laboratories.

The emphasis on the new schools like social sciences and economics created a need for new libraries. The New Bodleian Library was built in 1937–40 to the design of Sir Giles Gilbert Scott. More revolutionary is the planning of the post-war Law Library by Sir Leslie Martin and Colin St John Wilson, in St Cross. Since the Second World War, the growing importance of the scientific schools has been most tangibly demonstrated by the Nuclear Physics Laboratory and the Department of Engineering next door, the latter a most striking addition to the skyline. Oxford scientists have contributed

16 The Florey Building for the Queen's College, designed by James Stirling.

extensively to medical research, and this has largely been as a result of Lord Nuffield's generosity in the 1930s and 1940s.

After the Second World War, the emphasis on post-graduate research caused such an increase in graduates without college links that a number of new post-graduate institutions were founded, notably Wolfson College and St Antony's. Other colleges came into being for undergraduates, including older existing organizations achieving collegiate status and buildings. These included St Catherine's and St Anne's, both founded as associations of home students, and St Peter's Hall, which began as a private hall in 1928, and became a college in 1961. Most colleges have added to their buildings, making use of every available scrap of infill land.

Oxford has not been immune from the problems which have beset other centres in recent years. John Betjeman has described the three pre-war Oxfords: Christminster, the market town, Motopolis of William Morris, and the university. By 1945 the pressures created by these three conflicting interests had built up to an intolerable level. A post-war report described it as 'a city in confusion: a city whose apparent destiny, a destiny which had been followed over a period of seven hundred years, has been thwarted – thwarted largely by a bicycle in the backyard'. Thomas Sharp's *Oxford Replanned* (1948) put forward a number of solutions, based on now familiar post-war planning concepts, to solve the problem of protecting Oxford's historic areas, which he defined as one-tenth of the city area, from the effects of traffic. Although some of the more drastic solutions, like the notorious Meadows Road or the Merton Mall, were defeated by the sheer brazen weight of Establishment pressure from highly placed alumni of the affected colleges, working-class areas like St Ebbe's have been severely affected. However, Oxford now has its Outer Ring Road, and the modern equivalents of Pickford's waggons are kept away from Carfax. It remains to be seen how the development of the university and the shrinking of the British car industry will affect the future pattern of Oxford traffic.

17 (left) Bodleian Library: the Schools Quadrangle showing the Tower of the Five Orders: Doric, Tuscan, Ionic, Corinthian and Composite. Designed for Sir Thomas Bodley's library and built between 1613 and 1624. Beneath the canopy is the figure of James I, with Fame on one side, and the kneeling university on the other.

18 (below left) Schools Quadrangle, from the archway under the Tower of the Five Orders.

19 (below) Statue of the Earl of Pembroke (1580–1630), Chancellor of the University of Oxford when the Bodleian was being built.

20 (right) Top storey of the tower with the Stuart arms in the strapwork cresting; below is the figure of Justice.

BEATI PACIFICI

21 *(left)* The Old Clarendon Building, built in 1711–15 to the designs of Nicholas Hawksmoor, and paid for from the sale of Lord Clarendon's *History of the Great Rebellion.*

23 *(below)* Sheldonian Theatre, built 1664–9, to the designs of the young Christopher Wren. The Old Clarendon Building is on the right.

22 *(right)* Entrance from Broad Street.

24 *(left)* Window in the Divinity School.

25 *(right)* Old and new university buildings. In the foreground are the roof of the Radcliffe Camera and the Divinity School and the lantern of the Sheldonian Theatre. In the background is the Department of Engineering.

26 *(left)* Looking past St Mary's Church to Radcliffe Square, the Camera and the Bodleian.

27 *(right)* Rusticated arch on the ground floor of the Radcliffe Camera, used as an entrance until 1863.

28 *(far right)* Pinnacled gateway of the North Quad of All Souls College, begun in 1716 to design of Nicholas Hawksmoor.

29 *(right)* **All Souls College.**

30 (*left*) The sun dial in All Souls College, designed in 1658 for the Front Quad, but now in the North Quad. Attributed to Christopher Wren, who was Bursar at the time.

31 (*right*) All Souls College.

32 *(left)* Magdalen Bridge and tower.

33 *(below left)* New Buildings at Magdalen, from the deer park, designed in 1733, probably by Dr Clarke.

34 *(right)* Magdalen Cloister, part of the original buildings begun by the founder, William of Wayneflete, and completed by 1509. There is a cloister walk with rooms above on three sides, and the Hall and Chapel on the south side.

35 *(below)* Buttresses on the east side of the cloister.

36 and 37 *(above)* **Magdalen College.** *(right)* **Magdalen tower seen from Merton Walk.**

38 *(left)* St Swithin's buildings in Magdalen, designed by Bodley and Garner, and built between 1880–84.

39 *(below)* Magdalen cloister.

40 (right) A window in St Swithin's buildings.

41 *(above)* The New Buildings in Magdalen, probably designed by Dr Clarke.

42 *(left)* Tom Quad, Christ Church, looking towards the entrance to Peckwater Quad.

43 *(right)* Tom Tower, Christ Church, the upper part designed by Christopher Wren (1681–2).

44 *(above left)* Peckwater Quadrangle, Christ Church, designed by Henry Aldrich, Dean of Christ Church, and built between 1705–1714.

45 *(below left)* Canterbury Gate from Peckwater Quad.

46 *(above)* The Perpendicular Gothic vaulted ceiling to the Hall Staircase, built in the 1640s.

47 *(right)* Oxford Cathedral from the fifteenth-century cloister.

48 *(left)* Meadow Buildings, built in 1862–6 to the designs of Thomas N. Deane of Dublin in Venetian Gothic.

49 *(above right)* The old mill behind Magdalen.

50 *(right)* New College garden. On the right is the old city wall.

51 *(left)* Victorian buildings in New College; to the left of the tower they were designed by Sir G. G. Scott in the 1870s; to the right, by Champneys in the 1880s.

52 *(below left)* **William of Wykeham's Great Quad at New College; the chapel is on the left, and the hall on the first floor to the right.**

54 *(right)* The Cloisters at New College.

53 *(below)* **The late forteenth-century Muniment Tower, seen from the Gate Tower. The chapel is on the left.**

55 *(left)* New College cloister, built by William of Wykeham in 1400.

56 *(right)* New College chapel.

57 *(above left)* **Entrance to Worcester College in Beaumont Street. The chapel is on the right, the hall on the left and the library in the middle.**

58 *(left)* **The original** *camerae* **or lodgings for the monks of Gloucester College, dating from the fifteenth century. The buildings are now part of Worcester College.**

59 *(above)* **Hall window of Worcester.**

60 *(right)* **North range of Worcester College, 1753–9.**

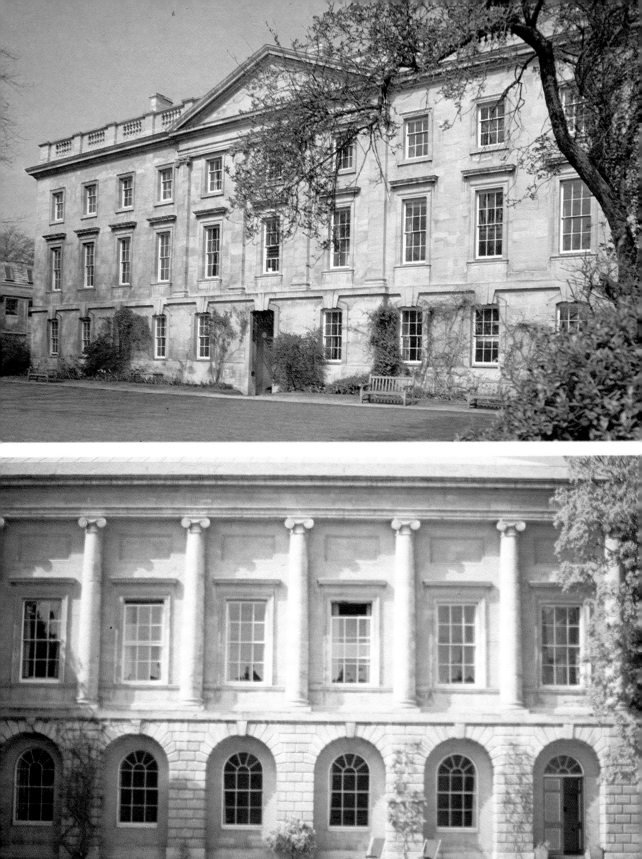

63 *(above)* Inside the University Museum; a dinosaur under a vaulted steel and glass roof.

61 and 62 *(above left)* The Fellows' building of Corpus Christi College (1706–12); *(left)* Oriel College Library (1788).

64 *(left)* **The Queen's College from the High Street; the gatehouse dates from 1734.**

65 *(below left)* **The North Quad at the Queen's College. The library (centre) was built in 1692–5.**

66 *(below)* **The gateway of the Queen's College, with a statue of Queen Caroline under the cupola.**

67 *(right)* **Entrance to the hall and chapel, the Queen's College.**

68 *(above left)* Canterbury Quad in St John's College, built by Archbishop Laud between 1631–6.

69 *(left)* The old library of St John's College.

70 *(above)* St John's College from St Giles.

71 *(right)* Front Quad, St John's College; originally part of St Bernard's College.

72 *(left)* Canterbury Quad, built by Archbishop Laud in 1631–6. The statue in the niche is of Henrietta Maria, the wife of Charles I.

74 *(right)* Front Quad, Corpus Christi College, founded by Bishop Fox in 1517. The sundial in the centre has a statue of the Pelican in its piety, which is the badge of the College, on the top.

73 *(below)* A corner of Canterbury Quad, showing the decorated lead drainpipe.

75 *(left)* The Fellows' Building (1706–12), Corpus Christi. On the left is the back of the library, built in 1604.

76 *(below left)* Fellows' Quad, the smallest quadrangle in Oxford, with the classical cloister on the right and the Fellows' Building on the left, both of 1706–12.

77 *(right)* The Gentlemen-Commoners Building of Corpus Christi, an addition of 1737.

78 *(left)* A stairway in Hertford College, designed by Sir Thomas Jackson in the 1880s.

80 *(right)* The tower of Merton chapel erected in 1448–9.

79 *(below)* The outside of Fellows' Quad, Merton College seen from Christchurch Meadows with the chapel tower behind. The chapel was intended to be the size of a priory church, but the nave was never built. Fellows' Quad, the first three-storeyed quadrangle in Oxford, was built in 1608–10.

81 and **84** *(left and right)* The Front Quad of Oriel College rebuilt in the seventeenth century. Above the porch *(right)*, rebuilt in 1897, are statues of King Charles I and King Edward II, with a Virgin and Child in the niche over them.

82 *(left)* The Rhodes Building of Oriel College, designed by Basil Champneys in 1908–11, and paid for by a legacy from Cecil Rhodes.

83 *(below)* The front of Oriel College (1620), facing Oriel Square.

86 (*above*) The Gothic gate-tower of Brasenose College, built by T. G. Jackson in 1886–9.

85 (*left*) Brasenose chapel, seen from the tower of St Mary's.

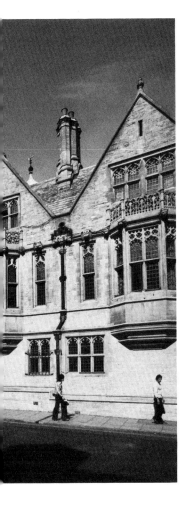

87 *(right)* **High Victoria bravura – a detail of Jackson's front to Brasenose, with St Mary's Church in the background.**

88 *(overleaf)* **Front Quad of University College, begun in 1634. Despite the fact that University College is the oldest in Oxford, these are its earliest remaining buildings.**

89 *(left)* High Street frontage of University College.

90 *(above)* The Front Quad of Lincoln College, fifteenth-century in origin, but with sash windows added later.

91 The sundial of 1719 in the Old Quad, Brasenose College.

92 *(left)* Exeter Chapel, built in 1854 by Sir George Gilbert Scott. It is in the French Gothic style, modelled on the Sainte Chapelle in Paris.

93 *(right)* The modest front of Exeter College towards Turl Street.

94 *(right)* Broad Street façade of Balliol College. Although it is one of the oldest colleges, it was almost wholly built in the nineteenth century under the great Master, Benjamin Jowett.

95 *(far right)* Although much restored, this is the only remaining medieval building in Balliol. In the background is Butterfield's chapel (1856–7).

96 *(left)* Old Quad in Pembroke College. Pembroke was founded in 1624 but incorporates one of the older Halls, Broadgates, which was much rebuilt later.

98 and 99 *(above and below right)* Keble College designed by William Butterfield as a memorial to the great Tractarian, John Keble. It was revolutionary in may ways, chiefly by being built in brick, but also in having incompletely closed quads, as the view of the east range *(below)* shows.

97 *(below)* The Front Quad of St Edmund Hall. The five-bay library building dates from 1680. The St Edmund Hall is the only surviving genuine medieval hall and became a College in 1957.

100 *(far left)* First Quad, Jesus College. This view of the north range shows the chapel and the Principal's lodgings. The College was founded in 1571, and has strong Welsh connections and a stalwart Protestant tradition.

101 *(left)* The shell-hood over the doorway of the Principal's lodgings (c.1700).

103 *(right)* Wolfson College, founded in 1965 as a graduate college for scientists, and designed by Powell and Moya.

102 *(below left)* The Cotswold Quad of Nuffield College, built complete with a chapel in the roof, and a broach spire, which doubles as bookstack.

104 *(below)* St Catherine's College

105 *(left)* Town Hall was rebuilt in the 1890s, to the designed of Henry T. Hare, in flamboyant Jacobethan.

106 *(above)* St Giles' and the Ashmolean Museum with the Randolph Hotel, designed in 1864 by William Wilkinson.

107 (*right*) **All Saints' Church in the High Street, built in 1706–8, and now converted to the library of Lincoln College.**

110 *(above)* Window detail from the main front.

109 *(left)* The Radcliffe Observatory, designed in 1772 by Henry Keene, but completed by James Wyatt in 1794. There are coade stone panels of the signs of the Zodiac, and the top storey is adapted from the Tower of the Winds. The building is now used by various medical departments.

108 *(left)* The University Museum, designed by Benjamin Woodward in 1853, to house 'all the materials explanatory of the organic beings placed upon the globe'.

111 *(right)* Sprandels in the University Museum, left unfinished.

112 *(left)* Punting is still the best way of enjoying the Isis and the Cherwell rivers in the summer.

113 *(right)* Nicholas Stone's gateway to the Botanic Gardens with Magdalen Tower behind. The Botanic Garden was established in 1621 by the Earl of Danby, who not only gave the site to the University, but provided a Yorkshire living to maintain it. It was very important to the medical school as it provided useful herbs.

114 *(left)* Isis House by Folly Bridge.

116 *(right)* A detail showing the balcony of Folly House.

115 *(below left)* Park Terrace, part of the Park Town estate laid out in 1853, and the first North Oxford development.

117 *(below)* St Michael's Church, dating from Anglo-Saxon times and one of Oxford's earliest churches.

118 *(right)* St George's Tower, part of the eleventh-century Oxford Castle.

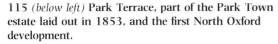

  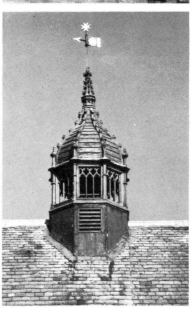

119–127 *(left)* Lanterns of Oxford (from right to left, top to bottom): Magdalen College, Oriel College, Wadham College, Lady Margaret Hall, Sheldonian Theatre, St John's College, Balliol College, Exeter College, Exeter College.

128–133 *(right)* St Hilda's College, Rhodes Building, University College, Jesus College, Lincoln College, Town Hall.

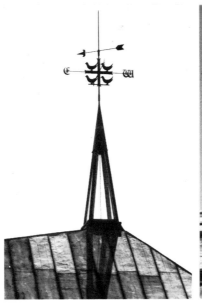

CAMBRIDGE

Medieval Cambridge

Cambridge, like Oxford, came into existence as a market town, strategically placed at a convenient river crossing between East Anglia and the Thames Basin. It was on the route of the ancient Akeman Street, and the Romans established a settlement there. It continued throughout the uneasy period of Anglo-Saxon settlement and Danish invasion, and soon after the Norman Conquest, the town gained its first charter. This gave it a valuable monopoly of the river trade as well as the right to hold its own court. By the mid-thirteenth century it was a corporation electing its own Mayor and bailiffs.

The religious orders were established soon after the Conquest, the Austin canons at Barnwell in 1112, and the fraternity of the Holy Sepulchre a year or two later. As at Oxford, the various orders of friars came to Cambridge early and played an important part in the life of the university. Some of the religious buildings survived the Reformation, like the medieval church of St Radegund's Benedictine convent, now part of Jesus College.

Cambridge historians, like those of Oxford, were long anxious to establish its origins in the mists of antiquity. A papal bull of doubtful authenticity was quoted to give it existence in the seventh century, while other claims made it a Roman foundation. Most modern historians accept that it was a product of the enforced migration of Oxford scholars during the five-year suspension of that university after the troubles of 1209. Some of the migrants remained to found a new *stadium generale*. By 1225 there is mention of a Chancellor, and there is evidence of a body of statutes by mid-century. It is not quite clear how much this was a model constitution, and how much a practical set of laws for the conduct of the masters and scholars. In any case it seems clear that by 1300 the university was well established, acknowledged as of equal standing with Oxford, its recognition confirmed by a papal bull of 1318.

In the thirteenth century most students lived in hostels or lodgings. The first college to be established was Peterhouse in 1284, combining two earlier hostels, but looking expressly to Walter de Merton's foundation at Oxford as a model. Colleges were essentially self-governing communities of 'post-graduates' intended to provide scholarships, support and facilities for graduates wanting to proceed to a degree in one of the superior faculties of law, medicine or theology. For a long time they catered for a minority, even of graduates, and it was the halls under the control of teaching masters which were the acknowledged communities of Cambridge students.

In the fourteenth century more new colleges were founded at Cambridge than at Oxford, seven being established as against four at Oxford. Many of these were later absorbed into other establishments, like the college of Michaelhouse, now part of Trinity, which was founded by the then Chancellor of England in 1323. Three years later the Chancellor, Richard de

Badew, founded a university hall, seen as part of the university, rather than as another independent college. It was not, however, very successful and had to be rescued by a local landowner, Elizabeth de Burgh, Lady of Clare, whose name the college took. The original buildings have now vanished but probably took the form of a four-sided court of a pattern becoming typical.

Great importance, was, however, given to Cambridge by the establishment of the first royal, almost the first official foundation. In 1317 Edward II founded King's Hall (again, later to be absorbed by Trinity) to provide for the education at Cambridge of choristers from the chapel royal. Twenty years later it was placed on a more secure footing by Edward III, who provided the first royal foundation at either university to cater specifically for students as well as teachers. This has been called a landmark in English university history since it set up an academic institution under the direct control and patronage of the Crown. Its head and fellows were appointed by the Crown, and it was supported by royal grant rather than by independently managed revenues. Its speciality early became civil law, emphasizing its role as a nursery for royal administrators.

Four more colleges followed within ten years: Pembroke (1347); Gonville (1348), founded by another local landowner, a Norfolk clergyman called Edmund Gonville; Trinity Hall (1350), established by the Bishop of Norwich, William Bateman; and Corpus Christi (1352).

Corpus, as the latter is usually called, possesses the oldest closed court to survive in Cambridge in its original form. In contrast to Merton, the prototype for so many Oxford colleges, it had no chapel, since the fellows worshipped in St Bene't's Church. This may have been due to the fact that this college was founded by two town guilds, those of St Mary's and Corpus Christi, rather than by an ecclesiastic or a member of the royal family who might have wanted to set this foundation apart from the townsfolk. The other buildings in the court were hall, kitchens and offices, library, Master's lodgings and chambers. The chambers consisted of a single large room for sleeping, with independent cubicles for study. It has been suggested that the model for this type of court was the plan of the Carthusian monasteries or Charterhouses.

There being no room within the walls for extensive foundations, these colleges were built outside the town, either outside the gates on the roads leading out of the town – an early form of ribbon development – or on the reclaimed area between the medieval Heighe Warde or high street and the river Cam. Very few colleges could emulate Merton or New College and erect a complete set of buildings at the outset, and at Cambridge economies seem to have been made by using existing churches as chapels.

The growing importance of the university and the colleges was increasingly resented by the townspeople who had suffered the invasion of an often disorderly population of students. In addition, the colleges were important landowners and when, in 1381, the peasants rose in revolt against local landowners, the colleges were also attacked. A mob attacked Corpus and also Great St Mary's Church, long identified as the University Church, and the repository of the University Chest containing valuables and muniments. The Mayor and burgesses joined in, burning university documents and seizing the opportunity to make the colleges and the university renounce their priviliges granted by the king. As was so frequently the case, the university gained immeasurably in the long run. When order was restored the privileges of the university were reinstated, with the addition of the important control over the sale of food and drink, a frequent source of friction between townspeople and students.

The fourteenth century saw the establishment of the first purpose-built university buildings. Originally, Great St Mary's had sufficed as a place of assembly for the university but in 1278 a piece of land was given for the building of a Divinity School. This was constructed between 1350 and 1400, and, with the addition of another wing in 1430, served as the university headquarters until the eighteenth century, being known as the Common Schools (now Old Schools). A library building was erected to house the books bequeathed by Thomas Rotherham, Archbishop of York, but was later demolished.

A number of new colleges were established at Cambridge despite the political troubles of the period, and indeed partly because of the religious unorthodoxy of Oxford where Wyclif's Lollardy had gained considerable following. The most important of these was King's College, founded by Henry VI in 1441, in conscious emulation of William of Wykeham's New College. It too was linked with a school, in this case St Mary's College at Eton, and was intended, unlike earlier Cambridge colleges, to have a cloister round its court. The townspeople were little pleased by the virtual sequestration of an important site between the High Street (now King's Parade) and the river. The first court was built next to the Divinity Schools but subsequent development has been south of the college chapel. The original foundation was for twelve scholars and a rector, but by 1448, in a document known as the 'King's Will', Henry VI set out a grandiose building scheme to house a much larger number. There were now to be seventy fellows and scholars, ten chaplains, six clerks and sixteen choristers. The only part of the scheme to be erected according to its founder's intention was the chapel, on which work continued until 1515. Chambers were to occupy the eastern and southern ranges of the court, with an entrance in the centre of the former. The western range was to house the public buildings, the library and the hall, with an adjacent smaller court for the kitchen, bakehouse and other offices. A number of distinguished architects worked on projects to complete Henry VI's plans but no grand design was ever achieved.

Henry VI's queen, Margaret of Anjou, was responsible for another foundation, now Queens' College, taking its name from not only her patronage but also that of Edward IV's citizen queen, Elizabeth Woodville. The Front Court was built very rapidly in 1448–9, to the design of Reginald Ely, the king's master mason at King's College. It remains one of the most perfect examples of a medieval court at Cambridge and is one of the earliest buildings to make use of brick, increasingly adopted as a more elegant substitute for the indigenous clunch. It also boasts a vaulted gatehouse, an architectural fashion which arrived in Cambridge during the fifteenth century and of which there are a number of fine examples.

King's Hall had already built a fine gateway in 1428, known as King Edward's Tower, and now part of Trinity College, while the original court of King's College, now part of the Old Schools, also had a great gateway. These became one of the hallmarks of Cambridge colleges, a feature rarely displayed at Oxford with the same panache, except in the case of the royal foundation of Christ Church. They were not only for show, their prominence being partly due to the need for security as the colleges lodged their valuables in them.

Renaissance Cambridge

The accession of Henry VII ushered in two hundred years of intellectual ferment, both political and religious, unparalleled in English history. Despite violent alternations of political and religious ascendacy which brought deprivation and often execution in their train, it was a period of growth in both numbers and learning in the universities. Cambridge, as the more progressive of the two, possibly benefited more from the stimulus, although her dons and scholars were far from uniformly behind both the Reformation or the Puritan opposition to the house of Stuart.

In 1485, however, it must have appeared that a period of peace had dawned after the turmoil of the Wars of the Roses. Henry VII continued with the great work of King's College Chapel, financing the final phase of building under the master mason, John Wastell, who had worked at both Canterbury and Peterborough. The fan-vaulted roof dates from this period (1508 to 1515), while the stained glass dates from the early years of Henry VII's reign. Both were miraculously completed before the Reformation began, and even more fortunately the glass survived undamaged through both the Edwardian reformation and the Cromwellian occupation.

The three colleges founded in the early Tudor period were all re-foundations of earlier institutions. The first was St Radegund's Convent, visited by Bishop Alcock of Ely and found gravely disreputable. He closed it down and on the site founded Jesus College for the training of secular clergy and teachers. The College inherited the chapel and some of the nunnery buildings, although most of the medieval work is now hidden.

The other two colleges owe their existence to Lady Margaret Beaufort, the mother of Henry VII, and her confessor, John Fisher, head of two colleges, Michaelhouse and Queens', who became Vice-Chancellor and then Chancellor of the University. Inspired by his advice, Lady Margaret re-founded God's House (later Christ's College), established in the 1440s as a modest establishment for the teaching of grammar school masters. The buildings were considerably extended with an important gateway bearing the foundress's arms, a large First Court, and lodgings for the foundress within the college. This court was re-fronted in the eighteenth century by James Essex, while G. G. Scott rebuilt the hall in 1876–9.

The formation of Christ's in 1505 went so well that Lady Margaret was persuaded to turn the Hospital of St John into a college also. Again the earlier buildings, including the chapel and infirmary, were taken over to form part of the First Court, which, together with its three-storeyed gatehouse, was built under the supervision of John Fisher from 1511. It contained both the Hall and the original Master's Lodging which was swept away in 1862 to provide an extension to the Hall. From the first it was a large college, containing in 1588 some 250 scholars out of a total Cambridge population of 1800. It was also traditionalist in that it retained the medieval provision for a geographical mix of students, and under its statutes half had to come from the northern countries. By the end of the century it had found another great patroness, the Countess of Shrewsbury, who financed the building of the Second Court, a four-sided closed court on the original Cambridge pattern. Better known as Bess of Hardwick, she was even more formidable than Lady Margaret: 'a woman of a masculine understanding and conduct, proud, furious, selfish and unfeeling. She was a builder, a buyer and seller of estates, a money-lender, a farmer, and a merchant of lead, coals and timber. She lived to a great old age and died immensely rich.'

Fisher also persuaded Lady Margaret to found a Professorship of Divinity, 1503, of which he was the first holder. He then persuaded the Netherlands scholar, Erasmus, complaining bitterly about the climate, the food and the wine and the general discomfort, to occupy the Chair. Erasmus resided at Queens' for two spells at Cambridge, and encouraged the New Learning in its many forms – radical theology, mathematics, Greek and the study of Greek writers and philosophers.

The suppression of the monasteries depleted the numbers of the students very considerably, and although some were converted into colleges, there was a real threat to the existing colleges from courtiers who wished to benefit from their suppression as they had from that of the religious foundations. However, Henry VIII took his responsibilities to Cambridge seriously, emulating his grandmother Lady Margaret in founding five Regius Professor-ships in 1540 for Divinity, Greek, Hebrew, Physic and Civil Law. Perhaps inspired by Cardinal Wolsey, his mentor in this as in so much else, he also founded a magnificent royal college at Cambridge. Here, as at Oxford, he was building on other men's work, but in both cases the result was the grandest foundation in the university. Trinity College absorbed two earlier foun-dations, King's Hall and Michaelhouse, which reverted to the Crown in 1546 under the act of dissolution of the monasteries. The new foundation was to be much larger with a master (a royal nominee even today) and sixty fellows and scholars, but it was to utilize the existing buildings.

Henry's daughter, Queen Mary, carried out some building at the college including a chapel for the combined foundation, but much of this disappeared when Thomas Nevile, who became Master in 1593, undertook the creation of the Great Court, which involved sweeping away the block jutting west from the gateway range, and taking down and rebuilding King Edward's Tower. He added a magnificent New Hall in the late Perpendicular style also to be found at the Middle Temple, and an open-ended court which bears his name, west of the Great Court towards the river. This was closed half a century later by Wren's Library, itself an innovation at Cambridge in its mastery of French Baroque detailing.

Magdalene College was another product of the Dissolution. It was a Benedictine house for monks studying at Cambridge, although it benefited from the generosity of the Dukes of Buckingham, bearing their name from 1483. The First Court dates from this period, and in the south range retains a set of medieval chambers, complete with study cubicles. The chapel is also a fifteenth-century survival but considerably restored in eighteenth and nineteenth centuries. The college was refounded by Sir Thomas Audley of Audley End in 1542, but not much building was undertaken until the end of the century when the Pepys Building was begun, although this was not finished until the end of the seventeenth century. Pepys's books were installed in the library in 1724.

Many colleges were feeling the pressure to build, since although the clerical students had largely disappeared there was a very much larger number of pensionaries, that is paying students not in receipt of scholarships who boarded in the colleges in varying degrees of comfort according to their parents' affluence. About one-third of the undergraduates fell into this class and, with the abolition of the hostels, of which there had been about a score at the beginning of the sixteenth century, there was a considerable need for the colleges to provide accommodation. This was indeed the period of greatest relative strength of the colleges as against the almost invisible university. College tutors and lecturers came to have more importance than university appointees, and this balance was not really redressed until the mid-nineteenth-century reforms.

Two more new colleges were founded in Elizabeth's reign. The Calvinist Emmanuel was founded in 1584 by Sir Walter Mildmay, a Chancellor of the Exchequer. It took over the buildings of the Dominicans or Blackfriars, which formed the Second Court. Despite its small size a new set of buildings was begun almost at once, to the design of Ralph Symons of Westminster, who was then working at St John's, Trinity and elsewhere. In 1668 Wren began work on the chapel, and in the eighteenth century much of the new Front Court was re-faced and brought up to date architecturally.

The second Elizabethan college was Sidney Sussex, founded by Lady Frances Sidney, Dowager Countess of Sussex, on the site of the Grey Friars monastery backing on to the odorous King's Ditch. The existing buildings had almost all been demolished, but enough remained to provide a chapel building, and work started at once on a court. This was of the newly fashionable three-sided plan, but most of the seventeenth-century work is hidden under Wyattville's re-fronting of 1821.

Dr Caius, a successful physician, who had studied at Padua and had been President of the College of Physicians, retired in 1556 to devote himself to founding a Cambridge college, in this case by enlarging the modest Gonville Hall. He added a court, but with only a wall and a gateway on to the street, with the intention of allowing air to circulate more freely, an important consideration when sanitation was elementary and plague an ever-present menace. His idea was widely copied and the earlier medieval plan of a closed court fell into disfavour. He also adopted another exemplary architectural features to remind undergraduates of their way through university life. The College was approached through one gateway symbolizing Humility; the student then passed through a new range of buildings into Caius Court through a gate marked on one side Virtue, and on the other Wisdom. Finally the student could leave the College through the Gate of Honour which led across Senate House Passage, towards Old Schools, where he would have taken his degree. The three gateways were well in advance of current architectural fashion, the Gate of Virtue (1567) particularly being one of the first examples in England of the newly revived classical architecture then fashionable in Italy and France.

No new colleges were founded until the beginning of the nineteenth century but existing colleges continued to expand. Clare Hall began

135 The Gate of Honour, Gonville and Caius College.

rebuilding its original court between 1638 and 1642, starting again after the Civil War in 1669, while Christ's erected its ambitious Fellows' Building in 1640–3, just before the outbreak of the Civil War.

Despite the puritan views of many Cambridge men, a number of whom, including John Harvard, emigrated to North America, most heads of houses supported the King. However, Oliver Cromwell himself represented Cambridge in Parliament, and the town's strategic importance across the route from London to East Anglia meant that it was garrisoned early in the campaign. Soldiers occupied some of the colleges, and at one point King's College Chapel was also used by them. Only Covenanters – supporters of Parliament – were allowed to remain in office, and many chapels and local churches were cleared of 'superstitious' ornaments and memorials. The student population fell, but returned in 1660, although a real and permanent fall in numbers took place at the end of the century, both at Oxford and Cambridge. At Oxford the student population rose from an average of 305 matriculated students in 1600 to 360 in 1660, and then fell to 295 in 1700 with a nadir of 190 in 1750. At Cambridge the figures were smaller overall but the burden is the same: 265 in 1600, 280 at the Restoration, 190 at 1700 and about 150 throughout the eighteenth century.

The Restoration was first celebrated by the building of Pembroke College Chapel, designed by Christopher Wren for his uncle, the Bishop of Ely, who gave it to his college as a thank-offering on his release from confinement by the puritans after eighteen years. It was Cambridge's first purely classical building, and was the first of several commissions to be given to the young Oxford professor. St John's erected its Third Court in around 1670, important in that it was the first set of chambers to be more than one room thick, a form of ground plan which rapidly became fashionable, replacing the medieval system of rooms with windows on both sides. Trinity erected its Bishop's Hostel to an altogether more old-fashioned design in 1669–71.

Cambridge is rich in seventeenth-century libraries, an indication of the wealth and activity of the period. The greatest of these is of course Wren's at Trinity. This was placed at the end of Nevile's Court, thus closing the view to the river, although Wren's original suggestion had been a circular building, an idea which was ultimately to be realized in the Radcliffe Camera at Oxford. The German bibliophile Conrad von Uffenbach, who visited it in 1710, found it:

> exceedingly handsome. . . . It could not be handsomer or more convenient for a library. It is very light, long and well lighted, and also highly decorated. For not only is the floor inlaid with white and black marble, but also the cases are all of oak, with excellent and very artistic carvings. It is very neat, made like little closets; – an excellent device because in the first place you can stow away many more books . . . and it is good for those who study there as they are not put out by seeing others facing them....[15]

Hanoverian Cambridge

'. . . We took a little stroll to view the town, which however, excepting the colleges, is no better than a village . . .' complained von Uffenbach on his arrival in 1710.

Hammond's map of 1592, which portrays all the college buildings very faithfully, gives this picture of magnificent chapels and stately gateways towering over modest and fairly uniform townsmen's dwellings 'more like huts for pigmies than houses for men'. The 'miry streets of this famous corporation' had struck other travellers, one of whom went on to complain of their narrowness so 'that should two wheel-barrows meet in the largest of their thoroughfares, they are enough to make a stop for half an hour before they can well clear themselves.'

Evelyn found the only redeeming feature was the market place with the fountain put up by Hobson, the famous carrier, who was one of a syndicate who promoted a new water supply in 1606. The low-lying situation was made worse by the lack of proper drainage and the stagnant nature of some of the watercourses, particularly the King's Ditch. There were frequent proposals to improve both the drainage and the navigation since Cambridge continued to be an important inland port until the arrival of the railways in 1845. Conservators for the river Cam were appointed in 1703, and in 1829 a report on the 'Present State of the River Cam' suggested various improvements including dredging which were duly carried out.

The most dramatic improvement proposed for the town was one which, in fact, never happened. Nicholas Hawksmoor, who had worked with Wren on most of his later works and then with Vanbrugh at Castle Howard and at Blenheim, was asked to prepare designs for completing the court of King's. He incorporated these into improvements in the baroque manner for the whole of the academic heart of the town. He did not attempt to alter the medieval plan of the town, but widened and emphasized the two main streets, particularly Trumpington Street, where he proposed to remove the small houses to make a series of baroque piazzas, using the existing church spires and college gateways to provide the *points de vue*. The two entrances to the town were to have piazzas with a widened bridge at the London end. A new axis was to be opened by clearing Petty Cury to provide a broad avenue from Christ's to the east end of King's College Chapel, another between the Old Schools and Caius to open up the front of Trinity Hall. The area in front of King's College Chapel and what was then called 'Chappel Yard' was to be cleared, and King's given a court to rival Trinity Great Court, with flanking buildings towards the river. A new block round a court was to stand where the Senate House eventually rose, while opposite the new King's Hawksmoor proposed a new public building, possibly to mollify the townspeople for the massive demolition of their modest homes and shops.

A modern architect, David Roberts, who has himself made a number of distinguished additions to post-war Cambridge, suggests that the proposals were too grand and too unifying to be welcome:

> At both Oxford and Cambridge he must have come to realize that the fellows and heads of colleges wanted neither palaces nor abstract architectural monuments, but houses. He must have discovered also that the university was an elusive body, whereas the independence and isolation of each college was all too apparent. The unity that he created was at variance with the twin dualities of town and university, college and university.[16]

In the event Cambridge got none of Hawksmoor's scheme and only part of a scheme by Gibbs (1722–30), where the Senate House was to be one wing only of a university complex to house a new royal gift of books, the university printing press and administrative offices. In 1754, Stephen Wright designed a fine façade to refront the medieval schools, but the university only obtained the whole Old Schools complex after King's College vacated its original court in 1829.

Conrad von Uffenbach found the state of the university 'very bad', and is disparaging about the state of many of the college libraries, which were the object of his pilgrimage. This was partly due to the fact that he came in the summer, when 'scarcely anything is done, both students and professors being either in the country or in London'. It is clear however that the eighteenth-century university was a place of great laxity and little learning. Undergraduates did as much or as little as they pleased. Even Henry Gunning, who was a scholar of Christ's, writes fondly of the wildfowling and fishing which could be done within Cambridge itself, while the shooting a few miles outside in the unreclaimed fenland was even more tempting.

Henry Gunning also describes the licence allowed to Fellow-Commoners who dined at the Fellows' table, unlike the humble Pensioners, who ate more modestly by themselves. Noblemen were distinguished by wearing a special gown, and during the eighteenth century this could be of any colour they chose – purple, white, green or rose-colour. As a further mark of respect for the aristocracy, until 1825 there was no requirement for them to take an examination before being given a degree.

136 A detail of the Gibbs Building, King's College.

The dons themselves were not always remarkable for their scholarship and a number of eighteenth-century professors held their chairs without giving lectures in their allotted subject. Although the colleges were at the height of their importance and all undergraduates had to have a college tutor, many of these were so deficient as teachers that the system of going to private tutors grew up. These were either resorted to *in extremis* just before the examination, or in the case of more ambitious candidates who wanted a 'Wranglership', one of the top places in the Mathematical Tripos, for a year beforehand. The two larger colleges, St John's and Trinity, dominated the university with their rivalry, while the smaller colleges found it difficult to provide enough tutors in different disciplines.

Evangelical Christianity, however, began to take a hold in Cambridge at the end of the century, first in Magdalene, and then in Queens'. Its chief 'low priest' was Charles Simeon, Vicar of Holy Trinity, and all his disciples were dubbed Simeonites. The university authorities were disturbed by the overtones of Methodism and radicalism in this movement, and when some undergraduates wanted to found a Cambridge branch of the British and Foreign Bible Society in 1811, the gravest apprehensions were aroused. Only the diplomacy of the Duke of Gloucester, then Chancellor of the university, who agreed to subscribe although not to attend the meeting, saved the day.

The eighteenth century abounds with reports of disorders of various sorts, either internally over some matter like the election of the High Steward or more frequently in 'Town and Gown' disputes. These were sometimes on the traditional Guy Fawkes Day on 5 November, or due to some extraordinary event as in 1820, during the royal divorce proceedings, when the town supported Queen Caroline and the university George IV.

The town's own politics were very disreputable at this period, almost complete control being held by the Mayor John Mortlock, from 1784 till 1816. He worked closely with the Duke of Rutland, and the Mortlock and Rutland interests controlled both the town and the university seat in Parliament until after the Napoleonic Wars. It was not entirely surprising that after the Municipal Corporations Commission had reported on Cambridge in 1833, the *Times* commented:

> Probably no judicial investigation into a public trust ever brought to life more shameless profligacy or more inveterate dishonesty, more bare-faced venality in politics, a more heartless disregard of the claims of the poor in the perversion of funds left for their benefit, . . . or a more entire neglect of their duties and functions as magistrates. . . .[17]

Some sympathy must be extended to the citizens of Cambridge, who were not exactly masters in their own town. As well as the habitual interference of local magnates like the Dukes of Rutland and Grafton, Lord Hardwicke of Wimpole Hall and the Earl of Bristol, a number of judicial and administrative functions remained with the university. The university only withdrew from participation in Sturbridge Fair in 1790 when it was in decline. It had been extremely important, partly as a market for cheese and other agricultural products, and also for Yorkshire cloth manufacturers and London iron-mongers. At the beginning of the eighteenth century London hackney carriages were said to come to Cambridge for the fair which went on for several weeks, to convey people from Cambridge. By the 1780s, the university's involvement appears to have been largely an excuse for the consumption of oysters and large quantities of mulled wine and sherry.

The university was much concerned over the possible effects of jollities of this sort on the morals and indeed on the health of the undergraduates, and retained the right to licence theatrical performances and the sale of wine until the end of the nineteenth century. There was also a power to 'discommune' or ban Cambridge tradesmen, under an arrangement by which local tradesmen were required to inform an undergraduate's tutor if he had incurred debts of over £5. This was a relic of the day when tutors were responsible for their pupils' debts and were supposed to prevent them running up large bills. Not unnaturally, the reformed corporation of Cambridge very much resented these powers as being in restraint of trade.

There was a further power which came to be even more bitterly disliked, and caused a public scandal in the late Victorian period. This was the proctorial power of arrest of women suspected of being prostitutes and found in the company of undergraduates. These powers had been granted to the university authorities by Queen Elizabeth, and they included the power of trial at the Spinning House Court by the Vice-Chancellor, and imprisonment there if convicted. At Oxford, the proctors had a similar right of apprehending 'any common prostitute or night-walker', but the women there who had been arrested by the university constables were tried in an ordinary court before local magistrates. The row between the town and university at Cambridge over this archaic power dragged on for several years, but was finally amicably solved by a new Act of Parliament (1894), supported by both parties, which abolished the Spinning House Court.

Despite the fall in the number of undergraduates and the general decline, the eighteenth century saw a certain amount of building. Much of this was caused by the deterioration of the clunch with which many of the earlier buildings had been constructed. Many of these were re-faced in ashlar as at Peterhouse by James Burrough in 1754, and at St John's by the local man, James Essex. James Burrough was an amateur who provided Cambridge with a number of distinguished classical buildings, although the major university commissions in the Old Schools (1754) went to Stephen Wright, a protégé of the politician, the first Duke of Newcastle, who was Chancellor from 1748–68.

It was James Essex who erected the famous Mathematical Bridge at Queens' in 1749, an indication of the growing importance of the Backs as the land to the east became built over. The original marshland was converted into walks, although Loggan's map indicates that some of them were already laid out with orchards and trees in the seventeenth century. The fashionable 'Capability' Brown was consulted in 1779 but, like so many schemes, his proposals for laying out the Backs as one pleasance were not adopted.

The one new college founded during this period was really an eighteenth-century proposal, the legacy of Sir George Downing, who died in 1749, leaving a provision that his money should ultimately found a new college. A generous open space, chiefly inhabited by snipe, was set aside for the building, but plans were not put in hand until the end of the century when Greek architecture was all the rage. Ultimately, William Wilkins was selected as architect, providing a scheme which was not only purest Athenian in feeling but also revolutionary in plan. As Dr Watkin points out, he abandoned the traditional closed court for a 'large and open campus-type plan incorporating houses for married professors', a compromise between traditional English and American practice adopted by Jefferson at the University of Virginia at about the same time. The whole project was never completed owing to shortage of funds, and the idea found no favour elsewhere amongst Cambridge conservatives.

Two other major neo-classical projects were realized in Cambridge, although many more were suggested. Both fall into the classical unreformed Cambridge period, rather than into the Gothic revival. As Cockerell declared when submitting his scheme for the University Library in 1829: '... the Grecian style is most appropriate to a classical Institution; is suited to all ages as maintaining the essential principles of beauty and magnificence in a superior degree....' The colleges continued to favour Gothic for their individual buildings, but university buildings were apparently seen as part of the enlightenment. Cockerell won the competition despite the opposition of Burton, who submitted both classical and Gothic designs, as did Rickman and Hutchinson. In the event only a small part, now the Squire Law Library, was ever erected.

The second building was the Fitzwilliam Museum, again the subject of a competition, this time won by George Basevi (1794–1845), but based on Roman rather than Greek examples. It was the first Cambridge museum, and was built to house the Fitzwilliam Bequest made in 1816.

Both these two buildings show the beginnings of the movement towards the increase in importance of the university as opposed to the colleges, a development which was to occupy reformers inside and outside both universities throughout the century following the Reform Bill of 1832.

Victorian Cambridge

The movement for reform in Cambridge took very much the same course as that in Oxford. Both universities suffered the inquisitions of the Royal Commissions of enquiry, both finally were coerced into reforms, nominally with their consent, often against the wishes of some of the older members.

An American undergraduate at Cambridge in the 1840s described the limited nature of the curricula:

> Mathematics are studied at Cambridge, and Classics at Oxford ... The Cantabs are stronger in Greek, the Oxonians in Latin, but they both read Classics; the Cambridge men however read Classics *and Mathematics*, the Oxford men Classics *and Logic*. This is the great pervading difference.[18]

Until the 1820s the Mathematics Tripos was the only examination for the degree of Bachelor of Arts, although degrees in Law and Medicine were also granted. The dichotomy between university and colleges was such that few undergraduates were encouraged to go to the lectures, even those given by Regius Professors. Instead they studied with college or private tutors, while the revenues available for paying the professors were often inadequate for attracting good candidates.

Most of the colleges were aware that reform was necessary and individual attemts at this were made. Whewell of Trinity, who was Vice-Chancellor and found the prospect of enforced government action on reform very distasteful, and persuaded Prince Albert to accept the Chancellorship on the death of the Tory Duke of Northumberland in 1845. Even royal patronage did not avert the dreaded reform. In a letter to Prince Albert in 1853, Lord Palmerston outlined the government desiderata; these included a better representation for the different elements of the university in its ruling body; the admission of larger numbers of students, whether they were members of colleges or not; the opening of fellowships to those who had not been members of colleges and a limitation on the time for which fellowships could be held (to improve the standard); and finally the transfer of some of the colleges' wealth to the general benefit of the university.

None of these objects could be achieved without legislation and in 1856, the Cambridge University Act was passed, after the bill for Oxford which had been carefully scrutinized by the anxious Cantabs. A new governing body called the Council of the Senate was set up which gave representation to members of the university who were not heads of Houses, and also limited the representation of any one college to two, reducing the importance of the two large colleges (Trinity and St John's). In addition, a body of Commissioners was, as at Oxford, set up to reform the individual Colleges.

These measures opened the way to a number of reforms including new triposes of physical and moral sciences and of law. The emphasis on scientific studies increased, doubtless assisted by Cambridge's traditional mathematical bent. The first tangible signs of this were the group of buildings erected to the design of Salvin on the grounds of the original Botanic Garden (1760–1852). In 1874 the Chancellor, the Duke of Devonshire, founded the Cavendish Laboratory which was intended to be a further encouragement to scientific studies.

Women's colleges were established in Cambridge in the 1870s, although Miss Emily Davies' Benslow House, the forerunner of Girton College, was established at Hitchin in 1869. By 1873 it had moved to a college which was being built at Girton, a village felt to be decently far from Cambridge. Newnham College came into being soon after on a site just across the Backs. Girton chose Waterhouse as their architect and Newnham the more comfortable Champneys, whose domestic neo-Dutch is perhaps more successful than Waterhouse's aggressive Mancunian Tudor. Although the women's colleges were initially welcomed at Cambridge, it was the Oxford women's colleges which were first accepted fully by the university authorities.

The only other college to be established in the nineteenth century was Selwyn College, which was intended to educate Anglicans. Its buildings were designed by that good Church architect, Arthur Blomfield.

Other additions had been made earlier in the century, starting with Rickman and Hutchinson's unrepentantly romantic Gothic New Court at St John's (1825–31), and Wilkins' Gothic New Court at Trinity (1823–5) and Library at King's (1824–8). The great Goths are abundantly, although not always happily, represented in Cambridge: Waterhouse more aggressive than usual at Pembroke; Sir George Gilbert Scott, magnificent if Oxonian at St John's; Salvin restored the Church of the Holy Sepulchre, predictably in a Norman dress. Most sympathetic perhaps is Bodley's work, to be seen in various college chapels and in Queens' College hall, but perhaps his most successful work was in the restored All Saints' in Jesus Lane, built in 1864. In much of his work he used the firm of Morris and Co. for glass and tiles and other decoration. The Gothic Revival is less well represented in Cambridge than in Oxford, due perhaps to its Low Church leanings. There is no work by Butterfield in Cambridge, and nothing by Burges or Street, although both were asked to prepare schemes for replacing Wilkin's screen at King's, neither of which were implemented.

The abandonment of celibacy for the heads of houses in Elizabeth's reign gave Cambridge a number of charming and original Master's Lodgings of infinite variety – from the half-timbered President's Gallery at Queens' or the battlemented stone front of Trinity, to Scott's new Master's Lodge at St John's. The effect of allowing Fellows to marry, which had led to the development of a whole new suburb in North Oxford, was less immediately marked at Cambridge. By 1907, however, a sprinkling of detached villas had appeared on either side of Grange Road. This suburb to the west grew slowly to accommodate the dons, while more modest housing went up between the town and the railway on the other side.

Gwen Raverat, the granddaughter of Charles Darwin, and one of the first generation of married Fellows' children, has left one of the most lively descriptions of Cambridge life in the last decades of the century. The university world was 'still small and exclusive. The town, of course, did not count at all.'

Dinner parties were frequent, and must have been slightly more complicated than diplomatic receptions:

> ... the Heads of Houses ranking by the dates of the foundations of their college, except that the Vice-Chancellor would come first of all. After the Masters came the Regius Professors in the orders of their subjects, Divinity first; and then the other Professors according to the dates of foundation of their chairs, ... the complications became insoluble to hosts of only ordinary culture. How could they tell if Hebrew or Greek took precedence, of two professorships founded in the same year? ... and their wives were even more easily offended.[19]

Even in 1891, no one asked the Master of St Catharine's, 'a little old man on his small black pony', because at the Mastership election 30 years before, he had voted for himself rather than for his opponent.

Undergraduates still amused themselves in fairly traditional ways although fowling and snipe-shooting became more difficult to find near Cambridge as the land round about was enclosed and drained. Even the Cambridge University Drag Hounds were bitterly resented by the local farmers, and an American visitor describes an affray in the 1840s when the hunt were intercepted by a gang of 'twenty fellows – ragged and dirty'. Most of the undergraduates, however, were happy with less contentious exercise:

> Every Cantab takes his two hours exercise *per diem*, by walking, riding, rowing, fencing, gymnastics, etc. ... In New England ... the last thing thought of is exercise ... unlike the Cantab's constitutional of eight miles in less than two hours. ... There is not a finer-looking set of younger men in the world than the Cantabs. ...[20]

Organized rowing came in in the 1820s in boats curiously heavy and broad by modern standards, but the river was also used for pleasure boating, although at some risk to health until the sewage was diverted from it in the 1890s. Queen Victoria, on a visit to the Master of Trinity, Dr Whewell, is said to have enquired about the pieces of paper floating down the river. He replied that these were notices forbidding bathing. This was in fact, not forbidden at all, and Gwen Raverat recalls the town boys bathing naked off Coe Fen and Sheep's Green, bathing suits being an invention of the uninhibited twentieth century. The conventional solution was simple: 'The Gentlemen were set to the oars ... and each Lady unfurled a parasol, and like an ostrich, buried her head in it. ...[21]

By the end of the nineteenth century organized games abounded and the map of Cambridge is full of cricket and football grounds for the various colleges, and indeed there are also a university skating rink and a cycle track. Bicycles, of course, were also used for transport, and dons would go out to dinner on them, taking their evening clothes to change into on arrival.

The Union Debating Society was founded in 1815 and, despite some trepidation on the part of the authorities, survived as a relatively sedate and well-conducted body, with its own premises designed by Waterhouse, near the Round Church (1866). The Apostles was a rather more exclusive club, founded in the 1820s, with a 'militant, masonic atmosphere, as of some secret society which was to reform the world' in the words of Harold

Nicholson. Amongst its early members were F. D. Maurice and Alfred Lord Tennyson, while in the Nineties it boasted even better known members in figures like J. M. Keynes.

Cambridge since 1919

The Armistice is a watershed in Cambridge history as in middle-class English life generally, although many of the changes were discernible before the death of Queen Victoria. The population of Cambridge rose sharply in the nineteenth century, from a mere 9,000 in 1800 to 45,000 in 1861, of whom some 1,500 were undergraduates. By 1911 there were 3,800 under-graduates in a population of about 70,000 in urban Cambridge, but the university no longer dominated the Cambridge economy; Chivers' jam factory had opened in 1873, and a decade later a precision instrument factory was started. In 1914 it was a university town, a shopping and market centre for the surrounding countryside, and a railway centre. Industry grew in importance in the inter-war years, while the diversification of government functions meant the establishment of a Regional Centre by 1948, leaving the university responsible for a mere six per cent of employment. The car overtook the railways, threatening the ancient street plan even in 1945, although post-war planners never seem to have anticipated the full horror of universal car-ownership!

This is the background against which the colleges have had to operate in the last fifty years and which has dictated the pattern of new building. The shopping needs of a large independent population have challenged the expansion of the colleges eastward into the town, and forced them westward, not only across the Backs but across Queen's Road and ultimately west of Grange Road. The distance from the traditional buildings along King's Parade and Trumpington Street has given modern architects greater freedom. Discreet experiment and architectural innovation abound in the most recent Cambridge buildings. Curiously enough, however, the most revolutionary building in post-war Cambridge, from the planning point of view, has gone up in central Cambridge. This is an eight-storey block for the ultra-conservative college Peterhouse, where the traditional staircase has been superseded not by the corridor but by the lift, a surrender to modern technology about which reservations have been expressed.

The first college to run out of room in the Backs was Clare, which commissioned Sir Giles Gilbert Scott to design the Memorial Court in Queen's Road in 1923–4, on the traditional Cambridge court plan which is open on one side rather than totally enclosed as at Oxford. Downing College, of course, failed to occupy its ambitious site, and even though it lost a large part to the university, had ample room for Sir Herbert Baker's 1930s additions, only completed in the 1950s. On the whole relatively little expansion took place between the wars compared with the post-war explosion.

Lutyens prepared a scheme for a whole court for Magdalene, but only one range was built. It is a Tudor gabled building with neo-Baroque ornament, rather less successful perhaps than his only major Oxford commission on a less promising site, Campion Hall. More significant is the other Magdalene commission of the period, Benson Court, where a group of existing cottages

137 Pembroke College, seen from Peterhouse: Wren's chapel.

were adapted as undergraduate accommodation by Harry Redfern. This was the beginning of a trend which has virtually dominated post-war expansion at both Oxford and Cambridge by colleges in the city centres. David Roberts carried out more conversion of older buildings for Magdalene in the 1950s, and Queen's College in Oxford has a most courteous discreet new quad behind houses in the High Street, designed by Marshall Sisson. Even one of the brand-new colleges, Darwin – a joint post-graduate venture by Caius, St John's and Trinity – occupies a converted building.

This is due partly to the recommendations of Sir William Holford, in his post-war *Cambridge Planning Proposals* in which he emphasized the importance of the 'contrast between the romantic irregularity of the shops and houses, for the most part small, and the large balanced masses of the Colleges and University buildings'. He expressed the hope that adaptation of the top floor of houses and shops to provide accommodation for students would be considered before total rebuilding. The trend towards public participation in planning has also probably had some influence on the matter. Colleges are no longer, as in the past, in a position to make architectural decisions consulting only their own prejudices and finances; the ordinary citizen of Oxford or Cambridge is now able to affect the actions of the colleges in a manner never before possible.

However, this has not prevented some very striking and often very satisfactory new building taking place in Cambridge in the last fifteen years. Up to 1958, the most remarkable new construction was the Erasmus Building by Sir Basil Spence at Queens', widely decried as spoiling the traditional view eastward across the Backs. A lost opportunity in the same class as Hawksmoor's scheme for a University Forum or Cockerell's University Library was the rejection of Walter Gropius's pre-war scheme for Christ's. In the event Sir Albert Richardson was commissioned after the war to add rooms for 90 undergraduates. He used traditional load-bearing bricks but abandoned the staircase for the corridor.

Two very successful post-war schemes east of Queen's Road have been added in the last fifteen years. The first is Powell and Moya's Cripps Building of 1963–7 for St John's, massive in scale as befits one of the two largest colleges in Cambridge. By one of the most successful firms of post-war modern movement architects in this country, best known for their Pimlico housing, the long thin zig-zag intervenes confidently between Lutyens at Magdalene and Rickman's New Court. A sign of the times was the architects' avowed intention of providing specially designed furnishings.

Most of the development has, however, taken place west of Queen's Road, where Martin and Wilson designed one of the largest additions, Harvey Court for Gonville and Caius, a massive complex with stepped terraces, which has been criticized for its urban design in a suburban setting, for the remorseless exposure of the undergraduates to public gaze, and for the extravagance of its construction. Corpus Christi too was hemmed in on its central site, and had to move out to Grange Road, where Philip Dowson of Arup Associates was commissioned to provide accommodation for research fellows, a new breed not always fully understood at Cambridge, too often seen 'as undergraduates in BA gowns', but here provided with spacious and secluded accommodation in Leckhampton House.

The Huntingdon Road is the home of three of the newest colleges, including the massive Churchill College, intended to add another 500 undergraduates and fellows to the Cambridge population. Richard Sheppard Robson and partners won an elaborate competition with a scheme of 20 courts designed on the staircase system, and also providing 20 flats for married members. Denys Lasdun and Partners are the architects for Fitzwilliam House, an older institution elevated to college status. The construction is of load-bearing engineering brick with clearly demarcated concrete floors, but fantasy takes over with the hall, with its vaulted concrete roof as apparently insubstantial as anything by Nervi. New Hall boasts a domed dining-hall, carried out like the rest of the college in white materials, brick and concrete.

In the town centre, two complexes mirror the polarization of function so fashionable in modern town planning. One is the new Lion Yard Centre, an improved version of the shopping centre cliché beloved of the 1950s, which destroyed a large part of Cambridge's remaining medieval street pattern. Earlier is the group of science buildings which stands on the old Austin Friars site, north of Downing and Pembroke Streets. This mushroomed after the establishment of the Natural Science Tripos in 1848, but is another example of lack of comprehensive planning by the University. Even less excusable is the development of the virgin Downing site acquired by the University in 1906 for development, and covered with a mass of scientific buildings catering for every type of specialization by a wide spectrum of architects, again without a master plan. Now many of these disciplines are moving out of central Cambridge because more space is needed.

Similarly, an Arts Centre was established in 1952 in Sidgwick Avenue, away from the historic University Centre round the Senate House, but in line with the Holford recommendations. This was to contain lecture halls, faculty buildings for Archaeology and Ethnology, English, Philosophy, Medieval and Modern Languages, a vivid illustration of the way in which the eighteenth-century dominance of college over university has been redressed. Hugh Casson won a limited competition for the master plan, and in Pevsner's words, the visual effect of much of the design 'is wilful or perhaps only playful, or one may be permitted to call it witty'.

In 1934 the New University Library by Sir Giles Gilbert Scott had been opened, a twelve-storey obelisk in pale russet brick, the tower designed on an axis with his earlier Clare College Court. It provides an interesting comparison with his New Bodleian Library at Oxford of three years later.

The Faculty of History Library by James Stirling, is one of the most aggressive modern buildings in England, let alone in Cambridge, exhibiting his passion for chamfering, and for using a hard red brick worthy of Waterhouse for the dominant material. A great glazed triangle, it occupies part of the Arts Faculty site and is even more difficult to relate to its neighbours than the overbearing University Library. 'Anti-architecture' it may be in Pevsner's words, but it is one of the most striking and successful of the post-war Cambridge buildings, a group which has done much to compensate for the banality of most inter-war building.

138 *(left)* **Punting by Trinity Bridge.**

139 *(right)* **The pediment of the Senate House from an archway under Old Schools. The Senate House was designed by James Gibb in 1722.**

140 *(left)* The Senate House.

142 *(right)* A view of the Old Schools building from Senate House Passage, showing the medieval building behind the eighteenth-century façade.

141 *(below)* Old Schools planned in 1754–8 by the distinguished amateur, James Burrough, Master of Gonville and Caius, but designed and built by Stephen Wright, architect to the Duke of Newcastle who was Chancellor at the time.

143 *(left)* King Edward's Tower, the oldest part of the Great Court of Trinity College. It was originally built in 1428–32 but was rebuilt 70 feet north of its former position by Nevile in 1599–1600. It is unusual for Cambridge towers in that it is made of stone rather than brick.

144 *(right)* The fountain of Trinity Great Court and the Great Gate. The fountain was rebuilt in 1715 to the original Elizabethan design.

145 *(above)* **Trinity Great Court.**

146 *(left)* **The fountain in Great Court.**

147 *(below)* **The clock on King Edward's Tower.**

148 *(right)* **The Great Gate of Trinity, built as the gatehouse to King's Hall at the end of the fifteenth century.**

149 *(overleaf)* **The north range of Nevile's Court, Trinity, completed in 1612.**

TRINITY COLLEGE
PRIVATE
NO
UNAUTHORISED
PARKING

150 (*left*) A view of Trinity College Library, designed by Christopher Wren and built about 70 years after the rest of Nevile's Court.

151 (*right*) The back of Trinity Great Court in Trinity Lane.

152 (*far right*) A doorway in Whewell's Court, built in the 1860s opposite the Great Gate.

153 (*below*) Punting under King's Bridge.

154 and 155 *(above)* King's College chapel, begun in 1446 and finished in 1515; *(right)* Clare College.

156 (*left*) King's College chapel from the south, with the Gibbs' Building (begun in 1724) on the left.

159 (*right*) Detail of the gatehouse and screen designed by William Wilkins in flamboyant Gothic Revival to be in sympathy with the chapel behind.

157 (*left*) Clare College bridge (1638–40) with the west range of the college overlooking the river. Both were probably designed by Robert Grumbold. To the right is King's Gibbs' Building.

158 (*below*) Clare College Old Court seen from the gate on to Trinity Lane.

160 *(above left)* The west side of Caius Court, probably designed by Dr Caius himself in 1565. On the right is the fourteenth-century chapel, the oldest in Cambridge, fronted in ashlar in 1718.

161 *(left)* Queens' College gatehouse from St Catherine's, dating from the mid-fifteenth century.

162 *(above)* The Mathematical Bridge at the back of Queens' College, designed by William Etheridge and built by James Essex in 1749.

163 *(right)* A window in Queens' College.

164 (*left*) President's Gallery,
Queen's College. It was built
in 1540 above the fifteenth-
century cloisters to
accommodate the President's
family when, after the
Reformation, the heads of
houses were allowed to marry.

165 and 166 (*left and right*)
Queen's cloister's with a detail
showing a window in the
President's Gallery.

167 (*left*) New Court, St John's, designed by Rickman and Hutchinson in 1825–31.

168 (*right*) St John's Gatehouse, built at the beginning of the sixteenth century, is one of the most splendid of college gatehouses. It bears the arms of its royal foundress, Lady Margaret Beaufort, mother of Henry VII.

169 *(above left)* Second Court, St John's College, built at the end of the sixteenth century by Bess of Hardwick.

170 *(far left)* A window in Second Court, St John's College.

171 *(left)* Cloisters in Third Court, St John's College, built in 1669–73 and still very provincial in style.

172 *(above)* The neo-Gothic New Court, a massive addition to St John's of 1825–31.

173 *(right)* The lantern, generally known as the Wedding Cake, crowning the centrepiece of New Court.

174 *(left)* Hutchinson's Bridge of Sighs, joining Third Court to New Court. The windows are unglazed but carefully barred to prevent undergraduates climbing into the College after hours.

176 *(right)* The cloisters of New Court, one of the most fantastic of Gothic Revival buildings in either university, despite its classical plan.

175 *(below)* Date on gable of Third Court indicating how old-fashioned some building at Cambridge could be even after Wren had started work at Pembroke. The arms are those of the Tudor founder.

o

177 *(left)* Pembroke garden showing G. G. Scott's New Building of 1878 (right), Caröe's linking block of 1907 (centre), with Waterhouse's Master's Lodge behind.

180 *(right)* Waterhouse's François I clocktower at Pembroke.

178 and 179 *(left and below)* The Classical revolution at Cambridge: Wren's pedimented chapel, with flaming urns *(below)*, designed for his uncle, the Bishop of Ely in 1665.

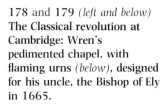

181 *(far left)* Old Court, Peterhouse, from the colonnades beside the chapel. The medieval court was re-faced in ashlar in 1754.

182 *(left)* The sixteenth-century library of Peterhouse, seen from Trumpington Street.

184 *(right)* The Burrough's Building in Peterhouse looking across Trumpington Street towards Waterhouse's building for Pembroke (1871–2).

183 *(below left)* Trinity Hall.

185 *(below)* Trinity Hall library, built in the sixteenth century. The small door on the upper floor originally linked the library to the Master's Lodge.

186 (*above*) New Court in Emmanuel College.

187 (*left*) Emmanuel College was founded on the site of the Dominican Friary, and much of their building remains in the Front Court concealed by later re-facing and rebuilding.

188 (*right*) Wren's chapel, designed in 1666, at right angles to the court rather than forming one side, and connected by open colonnades to the older buildings either side.

189 *(left)* New Court looking towards the gatehouse, with the library on the left, all designed by Wilkins in shallow Gothic in 1823–7.

190 *(below left)* Sundial in Old Court.

192 *(right)* Wilkins' chapel range at Corpus Christi replacing the earlier chapel.

191 *(below)* Old Court at Corpus Christi, the most complete example of a medieval college court remaining in Cambridge.

193 *(above)* Denys Lasdun's new building for Christ's, a sort of Mappin Terrace for students.

194 *(left)* Sundial at Christ's.

195 *(right)* Christ's College, the gateway to the Fellows' Garden.

196 *(below right)* The arms of Lady Margaret Beaufort, mother of Henry VII and a benefactress of Christ's, over the gatehouse.

197 *(left)* Jesus College cloisters.

198 *(below)* Entrance to Jesus gatetower from Jesus Lane, known as the Chimney.

199 *(above right)* Part of Magdalene College.

200 *(below right)* The Pepysian Library in Magdalene College, to which Pepys left his collection of books. The building was erected over a long period of time, this colonnade dating from the latter half of the seventeenth century.

201 and **202** (*top and middle left*) **Hall Court, Sidney Sussex College, showing the sixteenth-century buildings which were gothicised by Wyatville.**

203 (*below left*) **The range facing the garden, Sidney Sussex, built by J. L. Pearson in 1891 in neo-Jacobean style.**

204 (*above*) **St Catherine's court seen from Trumpington Street.**

205 (*right*) **Selwyn College, founded in the early nineteenth century for the education of Anglicans, was designed by Sir Arthur Blomfield.**

206 (*left*) Downing could have been one of the largest colleges since its founder's executors bought ambitiously. But funds have always been short and its growth slow. The two side blocks belong to Wilkins's plan of 1807, but the central block, by Sir Herbert Baker, is much later although it is similar in style. The hall is on the left and the Master's Lodge on the right, with lodges for the Downing Professors of Law and Medicine in the centre of each range.

207 (*below left*) An addition to Downing designed by Philip Dowson.

208 (*right*) Looking across from the hall to the Master's Lodge.

209 (*left*) Newnham College
was founded in the 1870s
and, for the first twenty-five
years, its buildings were
designed by Basil Champneys.
He provided them with robust
domestic quarters with no
quads but only ranges open to
the garden.

211 (*right*) Darwin College
was created as a graduate
college in 1965 by three older
foundations, Caius, St John's
and Trinity. It was established
in an already existing group of
buildings on the river –
including the house that
belonged to Gwen Raverat and
her husband.

210 (*below*) Girton College
was designed in neo-Gothic
style by Alfred Waterhouse
and, later, by his son, Paul.

212 (*below right*) Faculty of
History Library, designed by
James Stirling in 1965–8.

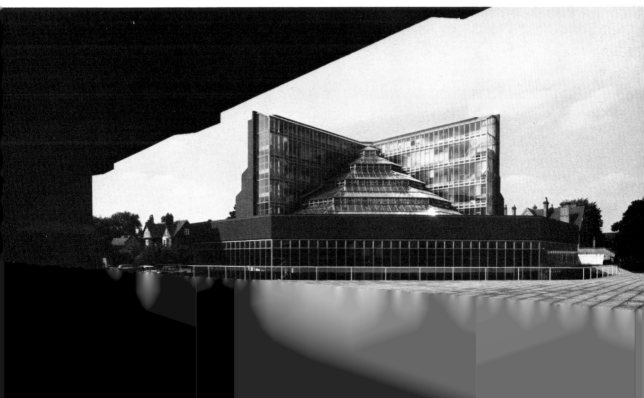

213 *(left)* Churchill College was founded in 1958 as a scientifically-oriented college for graduates. It has nontheless followed tradition by building in the old Cambridge pattern of courts, although the material is brutalist brown brick and raw concrete.

215 *(right)* St Bene't's Church. The oldest church in the county, with an Anglo-Saxon tower, it was used as a chapel by Corpus Christi College for two centuries until they built their own.

214 *(below left)* New Hall, the new women's college founded in 1954, built in gleaming white concrete.

216 *(below)* The new University Library designed by Sir Giles Gilbert Scott, and opened in 1934. It is seen from his Memorial Court for Clare College, built ten years previously. The tower serves as a book stack.

217 *(left)* The round church of the Holy Sepulchre, founded by a fraternity connected with the Holy Land in the twelth century. The round nave was extended and altered during the middle ages, but the church was restored in a scholarly manner by Anthony Salvin for the Cambridge Camden Society in 1841. He replaced the stone vault and restored the smaller original windows. Behind can be seen the aisles which flank the chancel.

218 *(above right)* Peterhouse College.

219 *(right)* The Fellows Building, Christ's College, built in 1640–3.

220 *(above)* Radio telescopes belonging to the university, outside the town.

221 *(left)* Fitzwilliam Museum, built to house the Fitzwilliam Bequest of manuscripts, pictures and books. Originally designed by George Basevi, it was built between 1830 and 1870.

222 *(right)* Bicycle stands near the Arts Site.

223 and 224 *(above)* Sundial in Queen's College; *(right)* The figure of St John on the gatehouse of St John's College.

225 *(left)* Gates of St John's leading on to the Backs.

226 *(right)* The Master's Lodge, Jesus College.

227 *(overleaf)* Old St John's Bridge with the back of the seventeenth-century Third Court behind.

228–236 (*left*) Lanterns of Cambridge colleges (left to right, top to bottom): Peterhouse, Queen's, Christ's, St John's, Gonville and Caius, Trinity, Christ's, Emmanuel, Queen's.

237–242 (*right*) Jesus, Christ's, Newnham, Selwyn, St John's, Pembroke.

243 *(left)* Trinity Hall library.

244 *(above)* View from the tower of Great St Mary's over Gonville and Caius into Trinity Great Court. St John's chapel is in the background to the right.

245 *(right)* Christ's College.

CONCLUSION

The primacy of Oxford and Cambridge is doomed. In another fifty years, or less, the most famous and influential of English universities will be London. This metropolitan drift is world wide ... The wealth of the metropolis, the abundance of its great cultural connections, its geographical convenience, and its attraction to foreign students combine to give the hegemony to Berlin over Halle, to Paris over Montpellier, to Rome over Bologna, to London over Oxford and Cambridge.[22]

Thus Michael Sadler in 1934, giving yet another awful prediction for 1984. Happily this prophecy seems likely to be unfulfilled. Certainly the University of London flourishes in her multiplicity of roles, and considerable challenge is presented by some of the newer English foundations where the specialization is formidable. But the changes grafted on to the older universities have brought about a form of renaissance and have not shaken the ancient order of things as much as might have been expected.

Since the 1950s they have weathered a considerable expansion in the numbers of undergraduates in residence, and a greater increase in research fellows and postgraduates. A number of new colleges have come into being to provide for more undergraduates and specialised facilities for postgraduates and the growing band of research students. The strength of the college

246 (*left*) **Greenhouses in the Botanical Gardens, Oxford, with Magdalen tower behind.**

247 (*centre*) **Winter scene on the Isis; motor boats laid up.**

248 (*below*) **Old Schools with King's College chapel behind.**

249 The School of Pythagoras, the oldest house in Cambridge, dating from about 1200.

tradition is demonstrated by the way in which the increase has been accommodated through them rather than merely through the provision of faculty buildings for the individual disciplines. A great liberalization in social mores and proctorial rules has also occurred, ranging from the relaxation of strict if nominal incarceration of undergraduates of both sexes after midnight, to the lowering of single-sex rules by colleges as diverse in their traditions as New College and Lady Margaret Hall at Oxford, or King's and Girton at Cambridge. With liberalization have gone many of the ancient social traditions enshrined in the great university novels, more particularly perhaps in the Oxford novels – *Zuleika Dobson, Gaudy Night* and *Brideshead Revisited* – but they are still recognizably the same institutions. Indeed, many of the mid-twentieth century changes are mere nothings compared to the more violent changes which were forced on them in earlier centuries, like the political changes of the sixteenth and seventeenth centuries or the traumatic moral and educational transformation of the Victorian period.

All these changes can be traced in the shape of the two cities today – in the planning of the colleges, the relationship between chapel and hall and staircases, in the very decoration of altar and stalls in the chapel, in the design of a hall for the most modern and informal of colleges, the inclusion of a chapel even in aggressively non-denominational colleges, and above all perhaps in the relationship of colleges and streets. Both cities are a matrix for architectural jewels of unique value, but a matrix which has gradually been devoured by its jewels, so that the academical buildings are replacing the mean streets. Yet for the inhabitants of Oxford, the bustle of Cornmarket is as important as the academic *largeur* of the Broad; the aridity of the remote campus, however beautiful, can be as destructive as the traffic maelstrom through which modern institutions like the University of Aston are approached. Here it is perhaps the college system which provides the protection for the scholar, enabling him to live remote from the town but within it. This book has been an attempt to portray and interpret this unique system, and the cities which it has created.

NOTES

1 C. A. Bristed, *Five Years in an English University*, Putnam, (1852) p. 1.
2 Statue of 1410, quoted V. H. H. Green, *History of the University of Oxford*, Batsford (1924).
3 Anthony à Wood: *Life and Times* (1665–6), quoted in Day-Lewis and Fenty, *Anatomy of Oxford*, Jonathan Cape (1938), p. 31–2.
4 Quoted in L. Rice-Oxley, *Oxford Renowned*, Methuen (1934) p. 117.
5 Joseph Trapp, Professor of Poetry, quoted in Green, *op. cit.*, p. 95.
6 Von Uffenbach, quoted in J. E. B. Mayor, *Cambridge Under Queen Anne*, Deighton Bell and Bowes (1911) p. 382.
7 Quoted in Green, *op. cit.*, p. 102.

8 Vicesimus Knox, *Essays Moral and Literary* (1782) quoted in Day-Lewis, *op. cit.*, p. 84.
9 Rev. W. Tuckwell, *Reminiscences of Oxford*, Cassell and Co. (1900) p. 248.
10 Ibid p. 3.
11 Ibid p. 2.
12 Mark Pattison to his sister, 10 November 1839, quoted in Green *op. cit.*, pp, 163–4.
13 Evelyn Waugh, *Brideshead Revisited*, Penguin (1979) p. 28.
14 C. Hobhouse, *Oxford*, Batsford (1939), p. 102.
15 Mayor, *op. cit.*, p. 125.
16 David Roberts, *The Town of Cambridge as it ought to be reformed*, privately printed (1955) p. 12.
17 *The Times* (16 November 1833) quoted in F. A. Reeve, *Cambridge*, Batsford (1964) p. 96.
18 Bristed, *op. cit.*, p. 136.
19 Gwen Raverat, *Period Piece*, Faber and Faber (1977) p. 78.
20 Bristed, *op. cit.*, p. 45.
21 Raverat, *op. cit.*, p. 108.
22 Sir Michael Sadler, quoted in Day-Lewis, *op. cit.*, p. 99.

BRIEF BIBLIOGRAPHY

Oxford

Betjeman, J.: *An Oxford University Chest.* 1938
Curl, J. S.: *The Erosion of Oxford.* Oxford University Press, 1977
Gaunt, William: *Oxford.* Batsford, 1965
Green, V. H. H.: *A History of Oxford University.* Batsford, 1974
Hinton, D. A.: *Oxford Buildings from Medieval to Modern.* Ashmolean Museum, Oxford, 1977
Hobhouse, C.: *Oxford.* Batsford, 1939
Pevsner N. and Sherwood J.: *Oxfordshire.* Penguin, 1974
Rice-Oxley, L.: *Oxford Renowned.* Methuen, 1925
Royal Commission on Historical Monuments: *City of Oxford.* H.M.S.O., 1939
Tuckwell, Rev. W.: *Reminiscences of Oxford.* Cassell, 1900

Cambridge

Bristed, C. A.: *Five Years in an English University.* Putnam, 1852
Gray, A. B.: *Cambridge Revisited.* Heffer, 1921
Holford, W.: *Cambridge Planning Proposals.* Cambridge University Press, 1950
Pevsner, N.: *Cambridgeshire.* Penguin Books, 1954 (rev. 1970)
Taylor, N.: *Cambridge New Architecture.* 1964
Reeve, F. A.: *Cambridge.* Batsford, 1964
Royal Commission on Historical Monuments, *City of Cambridge,* H.M.S.O., 1954
Steegman, J.: *Cambridge as it was, and as it is today.* Batsford, 1940

INDEX